MR. FOOD®
C O O K B O O K

OOH it's so GOOD!!™

CONTENTS

Dedicated to

They who put up with me, supported me, and loved me back

and to God — who did all those, gave me an insatiable curiosity for food, and most of all for bringing me to this season

Special thanks to Alan Roer and "Bobbi" Dworsky for their expertise and caring comments — Both of them superb.

© 1986 Ginsburg Enterprises Incorporated
First printing, November 1986
Second printing, May 1987
Third printing, October 1987
Library of Congress No. 86-091347
ISBN No. 0-9615951-1-6

Bolger Publications/Creative Printing, Inc.
3301 Como Avenue Southeast
Minneapolis, MN 55414
(612) 645-6311   (800) 328-4827

Introduction

I've put together in this book a selection of recipes and ideas that I've used on TV with a smattering of ones from my years in the catering business and even a few that I couldn't put on TV (because I couldn't condense the words or procedures down to a minute and a half, and still have them simply understood). Well, this is my chance to get them to you. The recipes I've chosen are either my favorites or your favorites — they all fit with our today life style — quick and easy, with readily available and economical ingredients — and all adaptable to your favorite tastes by adding or subtracting a smidgeon of this or a smidgeon of that. Oh boy!! That all sounds like a tall order — but it can work. If you just have fun in the kitchen or on the patio, with a little novelty, you can get that old-fashioned down home taste a lot easier than Momma did — 'cause Momma didn't have the convenience of all the things we have at our fingertips today (in both food and equipment). Go ahead — start your fun whenever you want, after all, that's my main reason for this book — to spread a little bit of happiness — just realize — you'll be a hero, and enjoy saying along with the eaters —

OOH it's so GOOD!!™

Ethnic Herb and Spice Chart

People ask me what my most important kitchen tool is. That's easy — It's not my favorite knife — It's not my favorite pan — It's a well equipped spice rack. It doesn't have to be expensive either. Have fun with it. It will take you anywhere in the world.

CHINESE
Ginger
Anise Seed
Garlic
Onions
Red Pepper
Fennel Seed
Cloves
Cinnamon

GREEK
Oregano
Mint
Bay Leaves
Garlic
Onion
Cinnamon
Fennel Seed
Black Pepper

INDONESIAN
Curry
Garlic
Red Pepper
Ginger
Cinnamon
Nutmeg
Cloves
Caraway Seed

SPANISH
Saffron
Paprika
Garlic
Onion
Parsley
Bay Leaves
Cumin Seed
Sweet Pepper

FRENCH
Tarragon
Shallots
Chives
Fines Herbes
Marjoram
Thyme
Black Pepper
Rosemary

HUNGARIAN
Paprika
Poppy Seed
Caraway Seed
Garlic
Dill Seed
Onion
Cinnamon
White Pepper

ITALIAN
Garlic
Basil
Oregano
Sage
Fennel Seed
Red Pepper
Marjoram

SWEDISH
Cardamom Seed
Nutmeg
Dill Seed
Bay Leaves
Allspice
Black Pepper
Mustard
Cinnamon

GERMAN
Caraway Seed
Dill Seed
Onion
Paprika
Ginger
Rosemary
Nutmeg
White Pepper

INDIAN
Curry
Cumin Seed
Coriander
Turmeric
Red Pepper
Black Pepper
Ginger
Cardamom Seed

MEXICAN
Chili Pepper
Cumin Seed
Oregano
Garlic
Onion
Coriander Seed
Sesame Seed
Cinnamon

MOROCCAN
Red Pepper
Cumin Seed
Coriander
Mint
Saffron
Anise
Cardamom
Cinnamon

From The American Spice Trade Association

iv

APPETIZERS

Some appetizers are fancy — some are down home — some are down home but fancy looking — but all of them are easy and the most popular ones from the show.

How they're served is up to you — garnishing and the platter they're served on are as important as the item itself. They don't have to be expensive, either. Sometimes a wooden cutting board can be more effective than a lace covered tray — so fit the appetizer to the party, the guest list and the mood you're trying to create.

And don't forget that the same recipe with a different spice can be a different recipe cause it's a little different taste.

Crab Dip for the Holidays

Blend together:	1 (8 oz.) pkg.	softened cream cheese
	⅓ cup	mayonnaise
	1 tsp.	prepared mustard with horseradish
	1½ Tbsp.	dried minced onions
	½ tsp.	seasoned salt
Fold in:	1 Tbsp.	chopped parsley (fresh or dried)
		dash of garlic powder
	1 (6 oz.) pkg.	frozen king crabmeat (thawed and separated into small chunks – or cut them that way)

Serve hot or cold. Makes 1¾ cups.

You can also mix the crabmeat with some less expensive imitation crabmeat to bring the cost down or even use all imitation crabmeat.

Chinese Cranberry Dip

Cranberries are not just for Thanksgiving!

1 Tbsp.	Dry Mustard
½ tsp.	vinegar
1 Tbsp.	water
1 (8 oz.) can	Ocean Spray jellied cranberry sauce
¼ tsp.	lemon juice

In a small bowl, thoroughly blend mustard and vinegar. Add water and blend until smooth. Set aside for 10 minutes. In a small saucepan over medium-low heat, stir cranberry sauce until melted. Remove from heat; stir in mustard mixture and lemon juice. Serve at room temperature with mini egg rolls.

It's only 4 ingredients and it takes no time at all! For a special treat try drizzling over pot roast!

Easy Clam Dip

Make ahead — keep in the fridge — throw in oven just before you need it!
Sauté 1 chopped medium onion in ¾ stick of butter or margarine until transparent. Take off burner and add:

1 (7 oz.) can	minced clams (drained)
1 (15 oz.) can	white clam sauce
1	paper strip of crackers - Ritz type (crumbled)
4 drops	hot pepper sauce
½ tsp.	oregano

Mix all together and put in oven proof baking dish. Bake in 350° oven for about 20 to 30 minutes. Serve warm as spread with crackers or cocktail bread.

> *This is the greatest at a cocktail party because you can make it the night before or that morning. Keep it in the fridge and a half hour before the party, throw it in the oven . . .*

Mystery Crackers

1 (11 oz.) box	"Sunshine" oyster crackers
¾ cup	buttery popping oil
1 packet	Lipton Cup of Soup "Cream of Chicken"
1 packet	Lipton Cup of Soup "Cream of Mushroom"

Pour the crackers into an airtight plastic container. Pour oil over crackers. Stir gently with wooden spoon. Sprinkle 1 packet of cream of chicken "Cup of Soup" and 1 packet of cream of mushroom "Cup of Soup" over crackers. Stir gently every few hours with a wooden spoon. Do not refrigerate. Enjoy anytime. OOH t's so GOOD!!™

> *You'll cause the biggest stir about your making that special cracker that nobody can figure out!*

Curry Dip

1½ cups	mayonnaise
3 Tbsp.	green onion (chopped)
3 Tbsp.	ketchup
3 drops	(or a bit more) Tabasco sauce
3 Tbsp.	honey
3 tsp.	lemon juice
3 tsp.	curry powder (or a bit more)

Mix together and let stand for at least 2 hours to marry flavors.

OOH it's so GOOD!!™

I don't ordinarily relish curry, but this is so unlike a regular curry taste, and so delicious, that you'll use it for every vegetable platter you ever put out. Nice conversation piece, too, because nobody knows what it is at first. The honey, lemon juice and onion combo has made this my favorite dip of all . . . and it's just mixing.

Gourmet Dips

1 cup	mayonnaise	or	1 cup	mayonnaise
⅓ cup	ketchup		⅓ cup	ketchup
1 can	tuna, finely mashed, drained well		6	mashed hard cooked eggs (boiled)
3 Tbsp.	wine (red or white)		3 Tbsp.	wine (red or white)
			¼ tsp.	pepper
			¼ tsp.	salt

Mix well. Chill and serve as dip or as a tomato style salad dressing.

Mix well and serve as a dip or as a rich Russian dressing.

Quick, easy, rich, simple without any cleanup and that's good for not only entertaining, but anytime!

Baked Party Dip

This will make your party the party of the year!

1 loaf	large dark bread unsliced
¼ lb.	butter
1	bunch green onions, chopped
6	cloves fresh garlic, minced finely
8 oz.	cream cheese at room temperature
16 oz.	sour cream
12 oz. (approx.)	cheddar cheese, grated (mild or medium sharp)
1 (14 oz.) can	artichoke hearts, drained and cut into quarters (water packed, not marinated)

Cut a hole in the top of the bread loaf about 5″ in diameter. If you wish, make a zigzag pattern to be decorative. Remove soft bread from cut portion and discard. Reserve crust to make top for loaf. Scoop out most of the soft inside portion of the loaf and save for other purposes, such as stuffing or dried bread crumbs. In about 2 tablespoons butter, sauté green onions and the garlic until onions wilt. Do not burn! Cut cream cheese into small chunks; add onions, garlic, sour cream and cheddar cheese. Mix well. Fold in artichoke hearts. Put all of this mixture into hollowed out bread. Place top on bread and wrap in a double thickness of heavy duty aluminum foil. Bake in 350° oven for 1½ to 2 hours.

When ready, remove foil and serve, using thin slices of warm garlic bread to dip out sauce.

The best part of this recipe is when all the dip is gone and all you have left is the bread which is soaked in all those delicious ingredients, you just break the bread up and pass it around!

Glazed Macadamia Chicken Wings

yields 40 pieces

4 lbs.	chicken wings
2 cups	orange marmalade
1 cup	macadamia nuts, chopped
2 Tbsp.	soy sauce

Remove and discard tips from chicken wings, cut each wing in half at the joint. Place pieces on foil-lined, greased shallow baking pan. Bake in 350° oven for 15 minutes; combine marmalade, nuts and soy sauce in a sauce pan; cook and stir over low heat until marmalade melts, about 2 minutes. Brush macadamia mixture over chicken pieces; continue to bake until chicken is cooked through, about 20 minutes, brushing with mixture and turning occasionally.

Keep brushing that mixture on the wings during the cooking. The more brushing, the better the glaze. Don't have macadamias?? Almonds will work great also.

Chicken Wings Marcelle

7 lbs.	chicken wings
1 tsp.	hot pepper sauce
2 cups	soy sauce
2 cups	orange juice
2	cloves garlic, minced
1 Tbsp.	Worcestershire sauce

Cut the tips off the chicken wings and put wings in a big baking dish. Mix other ingredients and pour over the chicken. Marinate for 24 hours. Bake in a 350° oven for 1 hour.

I keep basting them with the sauce from the pan quite a few times during the cooking hour. That's the only way they glaze well.

Chicken Wings — Buffalo Style

2½ lbs.	chicken wings (about 12 to 15 wings)
4 Tbsp.	(2 oz.) Durkee Redhot! Sauce (for hotter wings, use up to ¾ cup [6 oz.] The amount used in Buffalo.)
¼ cup	(½ stick) butter or margarine, melted

No-Fry Method: Split wings at each joint and discard tips; pat dry. Place on baking pan. Bake wings, uncovered at 325° for 30 minutes. Remove from pan and place in container. Combine hot sauce and butter; pour over chicken wings. Cover and marinate in the refrigerator for at least 3 hours or overnight. Turn several times.

Before serving, broil wings 3 to 4 inches from heat for 5 minutes on each side, turning until brown and crisp and brushing often with reserved marinade. Brush with any remaining marinade just before serving.

Deep-Fry Method (original Buffalo style): Split wings at each joint and discard tips; pat dry. Deep fry at 400° (high) for 12 minutes or until completely cooked and crispy. Drain. Combine hot sauce and butter. Toss wings in sauce to coat completely.

Don't have a thermometer? Yes you have — an electric skillet or a wok gives you controlled temperature.

Fry or no-fry method — they are still the rage! Serve them with celery sticks and bleu cheese dressing. (From Better Homes and Gardens)

Simply Portuguese

makes 4 servings

Do you like to dunk French bread and sop up all the gravy? This will be your new favorite!

2 (12 oz.) pkgs.	of sausage such as Linguica, Chorizo, Kielbasa, Knockwurst
½ cup	red wine - Portuguese is super!
1 tsp.	kitchen bouquet (or that type)
¼ tsp.	garlic powder

Slice sausage about ¼ inch thick and put in hot oven (about 400°) for 15 minutes. Remove from oven (careful, it's hot) and put in the combined, well mixed, remaining ingredients. Scrape the bottom of the pan and mix in well. Put back in the oven 10 more minutes, remove and serve with crisp bread for dunking and sopping. I sprinkle chopped green onions on just before serving.

OOH it's so GOOD!!™

This is probably one of the simplest dunking and sopping cooked dishes ever. Real old time throw together. Real old time family fun. (Like for a 'what should I make Sunday night?')

Salmon Mousse

1 (4 cup)	mold
1 (16 oz.) can	Salmon, red, flaked
1 lg. stalk	celery, finely chopped
⅕ can	olives, pitted
2 Tbsp.	lemon juice
3 Tbsp.	white vinegar
4 Tbsp.	sugar
2 tsp.	grated onion
2 tsp.	red horseradish
½ tsp.	salt
1 cup	water
½ cup	mayonnaise
1 (.25 oz. envelope)	gelatin*

Soften the gelatin in the water. Put on stove and dissolve on low heat. Add salt, sugar, lemon juice, vinegar, horseradish and onion. Take salmon, celery and olives and add mayonnaise and mix. Add slightly cooled gelatin, mix, mold, and chill until set.

*1 extra pack of gelatin for every 2 molds.

> *This recipe was one of our very first "hits" in my catering business — it helped make us — and it's still a hit! What a magnificent fancy delicious recipe — but so much simpler than it looks!*

Easy Egg Pizza or Soft Pizza · *1 medium pizza*

5	whole eggs
½ cup	flour
1 Tbsp.	grated parmesan cheese
1 tsp.	garlic powder

Combine all ingredients in blender for 60 seconds at high speed, scraping once with rubber spatula. Pour into a 12″ round or 9″ × 13″ lightly greased pan. Bake in preheated 350° oven for 12 minutes. Remove from oven, add sauce, cheese, and pizza toppings of your choice. Bake an additional 7 minutes, or until the cheese is melted. Cut and serve.

A shortcut way for egg crust pizza that's absolutely delicious! It's a family or company pizza that's tailored to your time as well as your taste!

Pizza Roll

1 lb.	pizza dough (frozen is fine)
½ stick	pepperoni
4-5 slices	Provolone (quartered)
1 (7 oz.) jar	roasted peppers
	dash garlic powder

Spread dough on well greased cookie sheet. Then lengthwise down middle of dough, line up pepperoni. Then, stack on top of that the slices of cheese and then the roasted peppers. Sprinkle it with a dash of garlic powder. Overlap edges lengthwise, enough to pinch dough together. Put in a preheated 375° oven seam side down approximately ten minutes. Turn the dough over and bake seam side up another ten minutes or until golden. Let cool and slice.

It's fast, it's easy, try this for Superbowl Sunday! (or really any Fun Day) Hot or cold — it's great both ways!

SOUPS

Here's a cross section of a few of the easiest to make soups that'll fit from fancy to family dunking.

There's summer soups, winter soups, and every season soups.

Have fun with them — use that spice rack too.

New England Fisherman's Chowder

makes 6-8 portions

¼ cup	onion flakes (or 1 fresh medium to large onion, diced)
3¼ cups	water, divided
2 Tbsp.	oil
2 cups	potatoes, sliced, peeled
2 tsp.	salt
½ tsp.	garlic powder
¼ tsp.	black pepper, ground
1	bay leaf
2 cups	milk
2 Tbsp.	flour
1 lb.	fish fillets, cut into chunks

Combine onion flakes with ½ cup of water. Let stand for 10 minutes. In a large saucepan, heat oil until hot. Add onion, sauté for 5 minutes. Remove saucepan from heat. Add remaining 3 cups of water, potatoes, salt, garlic powder, black pepper and bay leaf. Bring to boiling point. Reduce heat and simmer covered until potatoes are almost tender, about 25 minutes. Combine milk and flour; slowly stir into saucepan. Add fish. Simmer, until fish flakes when tested with a fork, about 10 minutes. Remove bay leaf.

You'll be making chowder in minutes that tastes like it was made right on the docks. Don't know what to do with that fish that was just brought home or the fillets that you forgot were in the freezer? This is the easy one that does it! Use any kind of fish from cod to snapper — and anything in between!

Beans 'n' Franks Chowder

A great taste for a cold wintery day. Simple, easy all-American dish — plus it's thick, hearty, satisfying and inexpensive.

1 (28 oz.) can	homestyle beans
4	frankfurters, cut in ½" pieces
¼ cup	frozen chopped onion
2 Tbsp.	butter or margarine
1 (1 lb.) can	tomatoes
1 Tbsp.	brown sugar
	few drops liquid red pepper
	seasoning

Measure out 1 cup beans from can, set aside. Mash remaining beans or puree in blender, reserve. Sauté frankfurter pieces and onion in butter or margarine until lightly browned in large heavy saucepan. Add tomatoes and liquid, brown sugar and red pepper seasoning. Simmer for 10 minutes. Add reserved whole and pureed beans. Heat slowly until soup is hot.

Thick and easy — great for dipping with bread.

Gazpacho

– A no-cooking Spanish cold tomato vegetable soup.

1 (46 oz.) can	tomato juice
1 cup	or so each diced cucumber, diced green pepper and sliced green onions
2 or 3	finely chopped cloves of garlic
6 Tbsp.	vinegar
4 Tbsp.	olive or vegetable oil
2 tsp.	salt
2 tsp.	Worcestershire sauce
	few shakes of hot pepper sauce (to taste)

Mix and chill and enjoy. I like to throw in a chopped fresh seeded and peeled tomato. But that's one of the options along with any fresh vegetables or your favorite spice such as thyme or rosemary or oregano or basil or dill. And if you're lucky enough to have fresh basil, chop it, add it and Wow! Wow! Wow!

This is fun to make when our veggies are in season 'cause it's like a cool walk in the garden and so delicious.

Hearty Fish Gumbo   *makes 6 servings*

1 lb.	fish fillets, fresh or frozen
¼ cup	margarine or cooking oil
1 cup	chopped onion
1 cup	thinly sliced celery
¾ cup	chopped green pepper
1 Tbsp.	finely chopped parsley
1	clove garlic, minced
1 Tbsp.	all-purpose flour
1½ tsp.	chili powder
1½ tsp.	salt
1 tsp.	paprika
⅛ tsp.	cayenne pepper
1 (1 lb.) can	tomato wedges, or whole tomatoes, undrained
1 (8 oz.) can	tomato sauce
½ cup	water
1 (10 oz.) pkg.	frozen whole okra, thawed
2 cups	hot cooked rice
	chopped parsley (garnish)

Thaw fish if frozen, skin fillets; cut into 1½ inch pieces. In a 5 quart Dutch oven, melt margarine; add onion, celery, green pepper, parsley, and garlic; cook over medium heat until vegetables are tender, not brown, stirring occasionally. Combine flour, chili powder, salt, paprika, and cayenne pepper. Stir into vegetables. Add tomato wedges, tomato sauce, and water; simmer 4 to 6 minutes. Add fish and okra; reduce heat, cover and simmer 10 to 15 minutes longer or until fish flakes easily when tested with a fork and okra is done. Serve with cooked rice. Garnish with chopped parsley.

Louisiana cooking at its best! Serve over rice with a crisp bread and summer salad!

Rhode Island Fish Chowder

Easy to prepare a day ahead! Go ahead — save some time and enjoy it even more.

6	slices bacon, diced
4 Tbsp.	butter
3	large onions, diced
4	cloves garlic, minced
3	stalks celery, diced
4	large potatoes, diced
	Fish stock or water to cover (about 4-5 cups)
4 (13 oz.) cans	evaporated milk
1 Tbsp.	Worcestershire sauce
1½ Tbsp.	salt
1 tsp.	pepper
¼ tsp.	Tabasco
1 cup	chopped clams (optional)
3 lbs.	firm fleshed fish, cut into 1″ pieces

Cook bacon until crisp. Drain and pour off all but 2 tablespoons bacon fat. Add butter to the pan and sauté onion, garlic and celery until soft, but not brown. Add potatoes and liquid to cover and cook about 5 minutes. Add remaining ingredients and cook until just below the boiling point. Cool and refrigerate over night. When ready to serve, heat thoroughly being careful not to allow it to boil. Serve immediately.

This is a true Rhode Island chowder. If you're not into meat, use a teaspoon of liquid smoke with 2 tablespoons olive or cooking oil in place of the bacon strips.

Easy Potato Soup

Try your own variation — maybe add some broccoli or grean beans!

4 Tbsp.	butter or margarine
1½ cups	diced onions
4 cups	large diced potatoes
1	coarse grated carrot (or 2 if desired)
2 cups	water
1 tsp.	salt
½ tsp.	pepper
1 tsp.	dillweed
3 cups	milk
2 Tbsp.	fresh chopped parsley (or dried)
	potato flakes (if needed)

Brown the onions in a saucepan. Add the potatoes, carrots, water, salt, pepper and dillweed. Cook on a low flame until potatoes are well tender, 20 to 30 minutes. Then stir in milk and parsley and bring back to the hot stage. If you wish to thicken it, stir in some potato flakes or buds. You can add frozen peas or broccoli at milk stage if you wish also. Enjoy.

> *This tastes like Momma's old fashioned potato soup. I do thicken it with potato flakes and I do cook it for 45 minutes so the potatoes are creamy. It's even better the second day.*

Corn 'n Potato Chowder

makes 6 cups

2 Tbsp.	butter or margarine
1 cup	onions, chopped
2 cups	potatoes, diced
2 cups	water
½ tsp.	salt
¼ tsp.	pepper
2 cups	fresh or canned corn
1 (13 oz.) can	evaporated milk
¼ cup	flour
½ cup	water
	paprika
½ cup	cooked ham, chopped (optional)

Cook onion in butter or margarine until tender and transparent. Add potatoes, 2 cups water, and seasoning. Cover and simmer for 15 minutes, or until potatoes are tender. Remove from heat. Stir in corn, evaporated milk and ham if desired. Blend flour with ½ cup water and stir into chowder. Cook, stirring constantly over medium heat until chowder thickens. (About 1 minute.) Sprinkle with paprika.

Crackers and cheese would just make this a whole light meal that will satisfy everybody! A hearty stick to the ribs kind of soup. Great for a cold winter night!

Strawberry Soup

makes 4 to 6 servings

1½ qts.	fresh strawberries or 2 (16 oz.) pkgs. unsweetened frozen strawberries
½ cup	sugar
½ cup	sauterne
1 tsp.	lemon juice
½ tsp.	vanilla
	fresh sliced strawberries (optional)

Thaw berries if frozen. In a blender container or food processor bowl, place half the strawberries and all the sugar, sauterne, lemon juice, and vanilla. Blend or process till pureed. Pour into bowl. Blend or process remaining strawberries; add to bowl and mix well. Cover and chill. Serve in custard cups. Garnish each serving with fresh sliced strawberries or mint leaves, if desired.

> *It's not French fancy — It's not expensive — But it sure looks and tastes it! No fresh strawberries?? Just use a couple of packages of frozen ones — It'll work just as well and then there's no hulling or washing. Great idea for a Sunday brunch or lunch!*

No Fuss Carrot Soup

5 cups	thinly sliced carrots (or your favorite vegetable)
1	large onion
2 cups	diced potatoes
	chicken broth as needed
	salt and pepper to taste

Sauté carrots with onions and potatoes until the onions are clear. Cover the mixture with chicken stock and simmer it for about an hour. Put it into a blender and spin until smooth, with a little bit of salt and pepper.

> *Got some carrots that are going soft in the vegetable bin?? This is what comes out to be a smooth, rich carrot bisque. Does that sound fancy enough? Maybe add a dash of dill? or basil? or tarragon? or a different one each time — Yummy!!*

RELISHES

Relishes are to the table as earrings are to the face — not necessary, but they sure dress up the looks and the taste. They're on the table with no work to serve them, as a filler to eat before, during, with and whenever. They give the table that full and ample look with a lot of economical color. Wow!! No wonder everybody serves them.

Here's a few that drew the most requests from the station — and I love every one of them.

Fresh Tomato Relish/20
Jiffy Corn Relish/20
Easy Pepper Relish/21

Cranberry Relish/21
Fresh Style Dill Pickles/22
Jiffy Mango Jam/22

Fresh Tomato Relish

4 or 5   good sized tomatoes,
chopped

Sprinkle and mix with 2 tsp. of salt (coarse is best but any type will work)

2   green peppers diced
1   good size onion diced

Drain off a bit of the juice from the salted tomatoes. Mix in the diced green peppers and onion and add:

1 Tbsp.   sugar   ¼ cup   cider vinegar
1 tsp.   dry mustard   ¼ cup   salad oil

Mix and chill. Readjust salt and seasonings. Enjoy! A dash of cinnamon or allspice might be nice also, it's up to you.

You know when you don't know what to do with all the tomatoes coming in? Well, here's one great way . . .

Jiffy Corn Relish

1 (12 oz.) can   whole kernel corn drained
or kernels from 3 ears of
cooked corn
⅓ cup   spicy sweet French dressing
1   carrot finely diced
⅓ cup   chopped green pepper
¼ cup   chopped onion
2 Tbsp.   pickle relish drained
2 Tbsp.   chopped pimiento
½ tsp.   celery seed

I could add ½ tsp. mustard seed. I could also leave out the pickle relish and add ½ tsp. sugar and 1 clove garlic, minced.

Combine all ingredients and chill for 24 hours.

Corn relish from those extra few ears of corn. The best part? No cooking! Yippee! Just mix.

Easy Pepper Relish

15	green peppers (sweet)
15	red peppers (sweet)
3	large onions
2 Tbsp.	coarse salt
3 cups	cider vinegar
1½ cups	sugar (or more if you'd like)
2 Tbsp.	whole mustard seed
⅛ tsp.	pepper
⅛ tsp.	salt

Seed peppers and coarse grind or fine hand chop peppers and onions. Mix in 2 tablespoons coarse salt and let stand in colander 15 minutes, no longer. While peppers and onions are draining, mix together 3 cups cider vinegar, 1½ cups sugar (more if you'd like it sweeter), 2 tablespoons whole mustard seed, ⅛ teaspoon pepper and salt. Combine with pepper mixture and simmer for 20 minutes. Cool slightly, put in individual freezer containers of your size preference. Seal well and freeze. Allow one container to chill in refrigerator and use fresh. OOH it's so GOOD!!™

With this easy, old-fashioned relish, you've got all the meat or poultry accompaniment you'd ever want. Steps above any pickle relish.

Cranberry Relish

1 (16 oz.) bag	cranberries (fresh or frozen)
1	apple (cored, but leave the skin on)
1	orange (small, seedless, leave the skin on)
1¼ cups	sugar

Put cranberries, apple and orange through a food chopper or processor. Add sugar, (more or less to your taste) mix well, and enjoy.

OOH it's so GOOD!!™

The taste of cranberries throughout the year!! So much better than cooked cranberry sauce — I use this like a fresh jam sometimes.

Fresh Style Dill Pickles

Fill a clean gallon jar with pickles or small cucumbers. Put in a cut half head of garlic (or 8 cloves, each cut in half. Don't bother peeling each clove.)

⅛ tsp.	alum
2	large shoots of fresh dillweed (bent well)
1 Tbsp. (heaping)	mixed pickling spices

In another gallon jar, mix a brine solution of 1 cup of coarse kosher salt and fill with cold water. (Mix it well) Fill the pickle jar to rim with the brine solution. Seal it well, put into your refrigerator for at least 4 weeks. Store in the refrigerator. Enjoy! OOH it's so GOOD!!™

Here's the old fashioned dill pickles that momma used to make. You can also put in a tablespoon of vinegar. I think it's better that way.

Jiffy Mango Jam

3 cups	ripe mango pulp
5 cups	sugar
1 pkg.	powdered pectin
1 cup	water
2 Tbsp.	lime juice

Sort and wash fruit. Remove skins and pits and chop in blender or food processor. Place mango pulp, lime juice and sugar in blender, mix well. Dissolve pectin in water, bring to a boil and boil for 1 minute. Add pectin solution to mango mixture, and blend thoroughly. Pour into jars or suitable freezer containers. Cover and allow to stand at room temperature 24 hours or until jam has set. Store in refrigerator a month or two or in freezer for up to a year. Note: If the jam is too firm for serving when opened, soften it by stirring. If it separates, simply stir it before serving.

Don't know what to do with mangos? But, you've run into a couple? Try this jam. It'll hold in the refrigerator for a month . . . how deliciously unique you'll be when you serve this.

SAUCES

Sauces make the difference — a barbecue is just grilled meat if there's no sauce. Spaghetti is just boiled pasta without a sauce to flavor it.

It's the signature and the identity for most every dish — it turns plain into taste sensation.

For centuries, professional chefs were acclaimed according to their intricate sauces.

Heck!! They don't have to be intricate and difficult — to prove it, here's a few that are as simple as can be.

Use them once in a while instead of your regular sauce for a break from the regular.

It sure makes things a bit more exciting.

Fresh Tomato Sauce/24
Deep Southern Hot Barbecue
   Sauce/25
Horseradish Sauce/26

New York Pushcart Sauce/26
Italian Light Sauce/27
Tartar Sauce/28
Cucumber-Dill Fish Sauce/28

Fresh Tomato Sauce

Here's what to do with those end-of-the-season tomatoes.

4	tomatoes (the riper the better), peel, seed and chop them
¼ cup	chopped green onion

Then to blender

½ cup	oil
2	peeled cloves of garlic
1 tsp.	oregano
1 Tbsp.	dried basil (or 3 Tbsp. of chopped fresh basil cloves)
1 tsp.	sugar
1 Tbsp.	wine vinegar
½ tsp.	hot pepper sauce
½ tsp	parmesan cheese

After blending, pour puree in a mixing bowl and add the chopped tomatoes and green onions. Use at room temperature over any variety of cooked pasta. And if you like the seasonings in the sauce to your own taste? Fine, use this as a base and go from there. Enjoy. OOH it's so GOOD!!™

Tomato sauce from the garden and no cooking! Add more seasonings if you'd like. Nice on a warm summer day or night.

Deep Southern Hot Barbecue Sauce

makes about 2¼ cups

2 Tbsp.	instant minced onion
¼ tsp.	instant minced garlic
2 Tbsp.	water
2 Tbsp.	olive or salad oil
1 cup	chicken broth or bouillon
1 (8 oz.) can	tomato sauce
1 (6 oz.) can	tomato paste
3 Tbsp.	white vinegar
2 Tbsp.	dark brown sugar
2 Tbsp.	parsley flakes
½ tsp.	ground allspice
¼ tsp.	salt
¼ tsp.	ground red pepper

In a cup, rehydrate minced onion and garlic in water for 10 minutes. In a medium saucepan, heat oil. Add onion and garlic; sauté 4 minutes or until golden. Remove from heat. Add remaining ingredients. Simmer, uncovered, 15 minutes, stirring occasionally. Use as a basting sauce over chicken, pork or fish.

If you feel like making your own distinctive BBQ sauce rather than doctoring up a bottle sauce . . . try this one and then next time doctor up a bottled sauce and see which you like better. Make a double or triple batch and use it for a few weeks.

New York Pushcart Onion Sauce

enough for 6 frankfurters (1½ cups)

2	medium onions, sliced ¼″ thick
2 Tbsp.	vegetable oil
¼ cup	catsup or tomato sauce
1 pinch	ground cinnamon
⅛ tsp.	chili powder
dash	Tabasco
dash	salt
1 cup	water

In medium skillet sauté onions in oil over medium heat, stirring until golden and limp, about 7 minutes. Mix in catsup smoothly, add cinnamon, chili powder, Tabasco and salt. Pour in water, stir. Bring mixture to boiling, reduce heat and simmer, uncovered, until onions are tender, about 10 minutes. Spoon about 2 tablespoons hot onion sauce over grilled or boiled frank in a bun.

On your next family weekend — perk up those old standby hot dogs with this old fashioned onion sauce!

Horseradish Sauce

½ cup	sour cream
½ cup	mayonnaise
2 Tbsp.	prepared horseradish, or 3, or 4, — (depending on how strong you like it)
1 tsp.	lemon juice

Mix together all ingredients in a bowl. Best if it sits in the refrigerator to marry the flavors. Enjoy, 'cause — OOH it's so GOOD!!™

Serve it with roast beef or use as a dip. Fresh, bottled or sauced — horseradish is IN!

Italian Light Sauce

Sauté lightly:
2 chopped cloves of garlic in a stick of butter and 4
Tbsp. vegetable oil.
Throw into the skillet over medium heat:

4 Tbsp.	chopped parsley
2 Tbsp.	chopped fresh basil or
	1 Tbsp. dried basil
2 Tbsp.	bread crumbs
3 Tbsp.	lemon juice
1 can	chopped anchovy fillets
	(undrained)

Heat through tossing lightly. Remove from heat. Let cool slightly and mix in well ½ cup sour cream. Serve over light foods such as fish, veal and poultry. OOH it's so GOOD!!™

You talk about a fresh smooth tomato sauce!!! This one's for light foods such as fish, veal or poultry . . . and there's nothing to making it. It doesn't have to be tomatoey to be Italian!

Tartar Sauce

1 cup	mayonnaise
½ cup	sour cream
½ tsp.	Dijon style mustard
1	medium onion minced
1 Tbsp.	finely chopped fresh dill
1 tsp.	finely chopped fresh parsley
¼ tsp.	salt
¼ tsp.	freshly ground pepper
	dash red pepper sauce

Mix mayonnaise, sour cream and mustard in medium bowl. Stir in remaining ingredients, mix well. Store covered in refrigerator up to 5 days.

> *This doesn't taste vinegary like the bottled ones. You can add more seasonings if you want, but start from here.*

Cucumber-Dill Fish Sauce   *makes 3½ cups*

2	large cucumbers, peeled, seeded and grated*
2 cups	sour cream
2 tsp.	lemon juice
4 Tbsp.	fresh dill, chopped (or 4 tsp. dried dill weed)
1 tsp.	salt
¼ tsp.	pepper

Add cucumbers to sour cream. Mix lemon juice and dill, and fold together into sour cream-cucumber mixture. Season to taste with salt and pepper. Great on poached fish. Serve with cold fish or as a salad dressing. OOH it's so GOOD!!™

*I use the grating blade on a processor blender

> *Also a great sauce over cold poached fish or grilled chicken. This is the rage in garden fresh tasting cucumber sauces.*

FISH & SEAFOOD

Fresh tasting fish used to belong to only coastal areas of the country. Now everybody can enjoy it fresh tasting because the modern methods of catching and processing fish at its source brings it to us fresh from the freezer as well as from the water — (and sometimes fresher) so fish no longer has to be strong smelling.

The today, light modern popular fish dishes are eaten more in restaurants than at home, but with the ease of preparing fish becoming more well known — in time that will change — and these recipes prove it.

P.S. Look in the future for the deserved increased popularity of these: Halibut and salmon from the ocean; and cat fish, Jamaiican snapper, trout, and salmon all farm raised fish from controlled clean water; imitation seafood — like crabmeat, etc., it's all made from really good fish. Plus — don't forget mussels — they're the best seafood value right now.

Ocean Garden Stew

or 4 servings

makes 1 generous quart

1 (6½ oz.) can	Bumble Bee chunk light tuna in water
3 tsp.	instant chicken bouillon
3 cups	water
1 (28 oz.) can	tomatoes
1 cup	quartered Dole fresh mushrooms
1	zucchini, sliced
1 tsp.	basil, crumbled
1 tsp.	garlic salt
½ tsp.	onion powder

Drain tuna. Combine bouillon, water, tomatoes, mushrooms and zucchini in soup pot. Add seasonings. Bring to boil. Reduce heat, cover and simmer 25 minutes. Remove cover and cook 20 minutes longer. Add tuna and heat 5 minutes longer.

This is so quick and easy. A little more or less of any particular item will make it your own special recipe. This will work with any fresh fillets cut into 2 inch pieces. Just throw them in the liquid and heat it 10 minutes instead of the five minutes with the tuna. Made in one pot — so no messy cleanup!

Baked Seafood Salad

makes 6 servings

2 Tbsp.	butter or margarine, melted
2 cups	corn flakes cereal, crushed to make 1 cup
1 cup	cut-up cooked crab, tendons removed
1 cup	cooked, deveined shrimp
½ cup	finely chopped green pepper
¼ cup	finely chopped onion
1 cup	thinly sliced celery
1 cup	mayonnaise
½ tsp.	salt
1 tsp.	Worcestershire sauce paprika

Combine melted butter with crushed corn flakes cereal. Set aside for topping. Measure remaining ingredients except paprika into medium mixing bowl, stir until combined. Divide mixture evenly into 6 individual shells or spread in 9″ baking pan. Top with cereal mixture. Sprinkle with paprika. Bake in a 350° oven about 30 minutes or until thoroughly heated.

Even though it's great as a main course, what a great hors d'oeuvre spread on crackers or toast triangles and is it ever luscious rich! Oh wow! They will swear it's a difficult, intricate recipe. You'll know better.

Seafood Casserole

makes 4 servings

1 cup	herbed bread crumbs
1 lb.	fish, cut into 1-inch pieces
¼ lb.	crabmeat
¼ lb.	scallops, cut into small pieces
¼ lb.	small shrimp
1 (10 oz.) can	cheddar cheese soup

Put all the ingredients in a casserole dish and cover with cheddar cheese soup. Bake 30 minutes at 400°. Serve with wild rice.

> *I make this the night before. Then all I do is boil the rice while I'm rewarming the casserole the next day. Instant meal — with hardly any cleanup at mealtime. Just one pot.*

Crispy Fried Fish

1½ lbs.	haddock, cod or grouper or the like, cut into thin strips
1½ cups	all purpose flour
1 Tbsp.	baking powder
½ tsp.	salt
½ cup	vegetable oil
1 cup	cold water
	oil for frying

Heat oil in a fry pan to 360°. To make batter, place flour, baking powder in a bowl and combine. Add oil, a little at a time, stirring constantly. (The ingredients should form a ball.) Gradually add water, stirring until the dough becomes like pancake batter. (If you want a thick crust, use less water for thicker batter.) Dip the fish strips in the batter, coating completely, and then in the oil, frying only a few strips at a time. When they turn a golden brown, drain on paper towels and keep warm in a slow oven. Return the oil to 360° and repeat with the remaining fish strips. These will stay crispy for quite some time. They may be served alone or with tartar sauce.

> *When you don't know exactly when they're coming home to dinner, this fish will hold crispy in the oven for an hour or two.*

Fish Scampi

2½ lbs.	boneless scrod or fillet of sole (if you use sole fillets leave them whole and only bake 10 minutes at most)
½ lb.	butter
4	cloves garlic, minced
2	scallions, minced, including green
½ Tbsp.	fresh dill or ¼ Tbsp. dried
½ Tbsp.	oregano
1 Tbsp.	chopped parsley
½ tsp.	salt
½ tsp.	pepper

Cut raw fish into approximately 2 oz. chunks (like huge shrimp) and place about 4 or 5 pieces in each individual casserole. Melt butter over low heat; add garlic, parsley, dill, oregano, scallions, salt and pepper. Cook on low heat for 2 minutes, then divide the mixture among the casseroles. Place casseroles in preheated 350° oven for 15 minutes. Serve with a rice pilaf, boiled new potatoes, or crusty bread, something that you'll be able to sop up that garlic sauce with. Enjoy.

This'll work with any white fleshed fish. It's so easy to make scampi. If you love garlic, this is your dish.

Puff-Topped Fillets

makes 4 servings

1 lb.	haddock or other white fish fillets (fresh or frozen)
¼ cup	dairy sour cream
¼ cup	mayonnaise
1 Tbsp.	chopped sweet pickle
1½ tsp.	minced onion
1½ tsp.	prepared horseradish
½ tsp.	paprika
¼ tsp.	salt
1	egg white
2 Tbsp.	melted butter or margarine

Thaw fillets if frozen. Rinse fresh fillets and pat dry. Combine sour cream, mayonnaise, pickle, onion, horseradish, paprika and salt. Beat egg white until stiff but not dry and fold into sour cream mixture. Season fish fillets with salt and pepper and brush with melted butter or margarine. Broil 8-10 minutes or until fish flakes easily when tested with a fork. Spread sour cream mixture on top of fillets. Return to broiler and broil 1-2 minutes or until topping is puffed and lightly browned.

Any fish fillet, fresh or frozen, ends up in a jiffy, looking and tasting like it came directly from the best of France and it's so easy. It's fish and dressing all in one.

Fish Peasant Style

makes 4-6 servings

2 lbs.	fish fillets	1 tsp.	parsley flakes
¼ tsp.	paprika	¼ tsp.	dried thyme
2 Tbsp.	melted butter	1 Tbsp.	lemon juice
1 tsp.	fennel seed, crushed	½ cup	dry white wine

Cut fish into serving size pieces. Arrange in a shallow baking pan and sprinkle fish with paprika. Combine remaining ingredients and pour over fish. Bake at 375° in pre-heated oven for 15 minutes or until fish flakes easily when tested with a fork. OOH it's so GOOD!!™

Turn any fish fillet into a fancy-tasting dinner in only 15 minutes!

Onion Stuffed Fish

makes 4 servings

1 cup	finely chopped onion	⅛ tsp.	black pepper
¼ cup	finely chopped celery	2 (1 lb. each)	fish steaks (fillet of sole)
⅓ cup	butter or margarine melted		salt to taste
2 cups	stale bread crumbs	2 tsp.	lemon juice
1 tsp.	salt		melted butter
½ tsp.	poultry seasoning		or margarine

Sauté onion and celery in butter or margarine until vegetables are limp and transparent. Add bread crumbs and cook until lightly browned. Blend in seasonings and lemon juice. Place one fish in bottom of buttered baking dish. Spread stuffing over the top. Place second fish over. Brush with melted butter or margarine. Bake in preheated moderate oven (350° F.) for 30-40 minutes or until fish is flaky. Do not overcook. Serve with boiled potatoes.

> *Here's an example of how to take fillet of sole or flounder and make it look fancy and different from your regular recipe. No rolling, no mess, and it's adaptable to any flavorings — not just these!*

Shrimp Creole

¼ cup	butter
1	medium onion, chopped
½	green pepper, chopped fine
1	garlic clove, minced
1 tsp.	salt
1 pinch	pepper
2 cups	canned tomatoes
1 lb.	cooked, cleaned shrimp
2 cups	hot cooked rice

Cook rice according to directions on box; keep covered and warm. Melt butter in skillet. Add onion, garlic, green pepper, salt, pepper, and tomatoes. Simmer 5 minutes. Add shrimp; heat only until shrimp are warm. Serve on hot rice.

> *Wanna add zucchini, fine — wanna add some pepper sauce for zing — or fresh tomatoes or basil or thyme — go ahead — there's no rules!*

Stuffed Fish Fillets With Dilled Potatoes

makes 8 servings

4 cups	mashed potatoes (instant)
2 tsp.	dill weed
1 tsp.	salt (or ½ tsp. garlic powder and ½ tsp. thyme for low sodium style)
8	fish fillets (approximately 6 oz. each)
⅓ cup	butter, melted

Mashed potatoes made from French's Complete Idaho Potato Granules, prepared according to package directions to yield. (Or mashed potatoes your style.) Thoroughly blend potatoes with dill weed and salt. Spread approximately ½ cup potato mixture on each fish fillet. Roll fillets and place in full steamtable pan. Brush butter over rolls and bake at 375° F. for 15 to 20 minutes or until done.

> *This is another one where you can be creative with seasonings to make it your own very special recipe!*

Tuna and Egg Bunwiches

makes 12 servings

10-12	hamburger buns, day-old, split	1 doz.	large eggs
2 cans	light tuna, drained, flaked	1 qt.	milk
½ lb.	Swiss or cheddar cheese, shredded	1½ tsp.	onion salt
		½ tsp.	pepper

Place bun bottoms in a greased pan. Portion tuna onto buns in pan, spreading to edges. Sprinkle cheese over tuna on each bun. Place bun tops, cut side up, over cheese. Beat eggs in large bowl. Blend together milk, onion salt and pepper. Pour about 1 pint over sandwiches in pan. Turn bun tops over, cut side down. Pour the remainder of the milk mixture over sandwiches. Cover pans with aluminum foil; let stand 30 minutes. Bake, covered, at 350° F. for 30 minutes. Remove foil; bake until knife inserted near center of pan comes out clean, about 25 minutes longer. Cut between each sandwich for serving. Serve hot.

From *Restaurant Institutions* magazine

> *Let's be honest — kids love bunwiches! And everybody's a kid!*

General Directions For Poaching
Whole Alaska Salmon *makes 12 to 18 servings*

Thaw 1 (4 to 6 lb.) whole salmon if necessary. Rinse salmon; remove head and tail if desired. I use filleted sides of fresh salmon. Wrap in cheesecloth leaving long ends on the cloth to serve as handles for removing from poaching liquid. Place salmon in large roasting pan. Squeeze juice from lemon half; pour over fish. Slice remaining lemon half; place over fish with 2 slices onion, 1 teaspoon salt and 8 peppercorns. Fold cheesecloth ends over fish so that no cheesecloth is outside the pan. Add enough boiling water to cover salmon. Cover pan with lid or aluminum foil. Bake at 425° F. or simmer on top of range allowing 10 to 12 minutes per inch of thickness measured at its thickest part or 8 to 10 minutes per pound or until salmon flakes easily when tested with a fork. Remove salmon from liquid using the folded ends of the cheesecloth as handles. But let them cool a bit because they're hot. Tongs would be more sensible to handle the cheesecloth. That's what I use. Gently remove skin while warm, unless you're using fillet. Garnish with lemon and cucumber slices and dill weed.

One of the most gourmet items you can serve is poached salmon! Serve it hot or cold — garnished with lemon and cucumber slices and dill weed! Your friends will say — Aren't they the fancy ones! And Ha Ha, it's really so easy.

Broiled Marinated Fish

4 or 5 (8-10 oz.)	fish fillets or steaks
	Mix together for marinade:
½ cup	orange juice
½ cup	soy sauce
3 Tbsp.	chopped scallions (white or green or both)
3 Tbsp.	cooking oil
⅛ tsp.	ground black pepper
⅛ tsp.	garlic powder
¼ tsp.	browning sauce such as Kitchen Bouquet or Gravy Master or Maggi
	Add any of the below spices:
1 tsp.	dried basil, or
¼ tsp.	ground ginger, or
1 tsp.	dried thyme, or
¼ tsp.	nutmeg, or
1 tsp.	chili powder, or
	your favorite seasoning

Pour marinade over the fish steaks or fillets in a baking pan, cover it with foil, put it in the refrigerator and leave it there for 2 to 4 hours . . . (depending on how strong you want the fish penetrated) — not any more, I'd say. Then drain the fish reserving the marinade. Broil fish about 10 minutes per inch of thickness, basting it with the marinade occasionally, for darker color if you wish. I warm the marinade in a saucepan on the stove while the fish is broiling and spoon some over the finished dish. Mmm, mmm!

Change your spices to make it different each time! With the emphasis on lighter foods, this dish fills the bill!

CHICKEN & TURKEY

In the last few years poultry has grown so much in popularity that there's an insatiable desire for more and more new ways with it.

What used to be a weekend or holiday treat has become an every day affordable treat — while it fits light, modern and easy — that's a nice situation for us.

I don't know which one it was, the Fancy Fast Chicken, the Chicken with Orange, or the Oven-Fried Chicken with Honey-Butter Sauce that was the most requested chicken recipe, but those and the others included in this section were, (and still are) the most requested of all the poultry dishes we've done on TV.

All easy as pie — chicken and turkey.

Skewered Chicken

makes 6 to 8 servings

3	medium chicken breasts split, skinned and boned
¼ cup	soy sauce
3 Tbsp.	dry white wine
2 Tbsp.	lemon juice
2 Tbsp.	cooking oil
¾ tsp.	fine herbs, crushed
½ tsp.	grated gingerroot
1	clove garlic, minced
¼ tsp.	onion powder
	dash pepper

Cut chicken into strips, 1¼ inch wide and ¼ inch thick. Thread strips loosely onto 6 to 8 skewers. Place skewers in two layers in a 12 × 7½ × 2″ baking dish. Combine remaining ingredients. Pour over chicken. Cover and chill 2 to 3 hours. Drain. Grill over hot coals 3 to 4 minutes per side. Garnish with cherry tomatoes and parsley, if desired.

This can be worked with chicken chunks — You don't need strips — nice marinade that's absorbed right into the chicken. Mmmm! Mmmm!

Oven Barbecued Chicken

makes 6 servings

2½ - 3 lbs.	chicken pieces
	garlic salt
½ cup	each: orange marmalade
	and ketchup
¼ cup	A-1 steak sauce
1 Tbsp.	lemon juice

Sprinkle both sides of chicken with garlic salt, place in shallow baking pan. Combine remaining ingredients. Baste chicken generously with sauce. Bake in preheated 400°F oven 1 hour. While baking, frequently turn and baste chicken.

> *Easy, easy — You can use a bottled BBQ sauce instead of the ketchup and steak sauce if you want. In case it rains, you can still have a BBQ.*

Easy Cacciatore

To every 3 lbs. chicken: cook in enough oil to brown. Brown chicken in oil and remove from pan; slice an onion and cook in drippings until soft. Then add to pan:

1 can	tomatoes
½ cup	minced parsley
1 tsp.	basil
1 tsp.	salt
1	minced clove garlic
¼ tsp.	pepper

Put chicken back in pan and let it simmer for about 40 minutes uncovered, turning the chicken once in a while.

OOH it's so GOOD!!™

> *This is one easy cacciatore recipe. It's fast and delicious — real Italian homestyle.*

Mustard Chicken

makes 12 servings

4 (2 ½ lbs each)	chickens, cut into eighths
¾ cup	oil
1 Tbsp.	salt
½ tsp.	onion powder
½ tsp.	red pepper, ground
3 Tbsp.	mustard, powdered
3 Tbsp.	water, warm
¾ cup	butter, melted
⅓ cup	white wine, dry
1 tsp.	lemon juice
1½ cups	bread crumbs (dry)

Mix together oil, salt, onion powder and pepper; dip chicken in oil. Place in shallow pan, bake at 375°F until tender, about 35 minutes. Mix mustard with water; let stand 10 minutes; add butter, wine and lemon juice; mix well. Brush baked chicken with mustard mixture; coat with bread crumbs. Place chicken on racks in broiler pans; broil 6 inches from heat until browned, about 2 minutes on each side.

I add a tablespoon of sugar to this for an easy, smooth taste.

Teriyaki Chicken

makes 6 servings

½ cup	reconstituted lemon juice
⅓ cup	soy sauce
⅓ cup	vegetable oil
¼ cup	chili sauce
½ tsp.	pepper
½ tsp.	garlic powder
5 lbs.	chicken fryer parts

Combine all ingredients and pour over chicken parts and put in refrigerator overnight. Put on the grill or bake in 350° oven for about 1½ hours or until golden brown. Occasionally during cooking, baste it with the juices.

Don't spend time away from your guests at the grill doing the barbecuing — you can bake it in the oven!

Honey Barbecued Chicken *makes 4 servings*

1 (2½ to 3 lb.)	chicken, cut into serving-size pieces
3 Tbsp.	salad oil
¼ cup	honey
2 Tbsp.	Lea & Perrins Worcestershire sauce
1½ Tbsp.	lemon juice
1½ tsp.	salt
1 tsp.	onion powder
1½ tsp.	garlic powder

Brush chicken pieces with oil. Arrange chicken on rack in broiler pan. Place under preheated hot broiler and broil for 15 minutes, turning once. Meanwhile, combine remaining ingredients; mix well. Baste each chicken piece with honey mixture several times, turning occasionally. Broil 30 to 40 minutes longer or until chicken is tender.

We're always looking for a new way with chicken. Well, this needs a few more bastings and turning than usual, but its slightly tart 'n sweet flavor is nice for a change. If you'd like to sprinkle it with your favorite spice, go ahead — make your own creation.

Louisiana Chicken

makes 8 servings

¼ cup	salad oil
2 (2 to 2½ lb.)	broiler fryers, cut up
½ cup	all purpose flour
4	medium celery stalks, thinly sliced
3	medium green peppers, cut into thin strips
2	medium onions, diced
2	chicken-flavored bouillon cubes or envelopes
3 cups	water
2¼ tsp.	salt
½ tsp.	hot pepper sauce

About 1½ hours before serving: in 12 inch skillet over medium heat, in hot salad oil, cook chicken, a few pieces at a time, until browned on all sides. Remove chicken pieces as they brown to 4 or 5 quart casserole. Into hot drippings in skillet over medium heat, stir flour; cook, stirring constantly, until flour is dark brown. Add celery, green peppers, and onions. Cook until vegetables are tender, stirring frequently. Stir in bouillon, water, salt and hot pepper sauce. Over high heat, heat mixture to boiling. Pre-heat oven to 350°F. Pour sauce over chicken in casserole. Bake casserole uncovered 45 minutes or until chicken is fork tender, occasionally basting chicken with sauce in casserole; skim off fat from sauce.

Chicken and gravy all in one. Tastes like the new rage in food — good down home American. It's Louisiana-style cooking at its best.

Chicken Beer Bake

makes 3 to 6 servings

3	whole chicken breasts, split
5 Tbsp.	all purpose flour
	salt and pepper to taste (¼ tsp.)
2 cans	cream of chicken soup undiluted
1 Tbsp.	soy sauce
¼ cup	toasted slivered almonds
½ cup	beer
1 (3 oz.) can	mushrooms, drained, or ⅓ cup cooked, sliced mushrooms

Remove skin from chicken, rinse under cold water and dry well with absorbent towel. Combine flour, salt and pepper in a paper bag and shake the chicken breasts individually in the bag to coat. Place the breasts in a shallow pan; combine soup, soy sauce, almonds, beer and mushrooms; pour that over the breasts. Bake uncovered at 350° for one hour, basting occasionally. Served over rice to sop up that gravy. Yummee.

Don't know what I like more, the chicken or the gravy or how easy it is to make. An easy to do recipe that can be used for company or the home folks.

Tasty Taco Chicken Grill

1	broiler-fryer chicken cut in parts
1	small onion, minced
1 (8 oz.) can	Spanish-style tomato sauce
1 (4 oz.) can	taco sauce
¼ cup	molasses
2 Tbsp.	vinegar
1 Tbsp.	cooking oil
1 tsp.	salt
½ tsp.	oregano leaves
⅛ tsp.	pepper
½ cup	grated Monterey Jack cheese (optional)

Lay out broiler fryer parts in baking dish and bake in 350° oven for 40 minutes. Cool them a bit and pour sauce (method below) over the chicken, cover and marinate in refrigerator for at least an hour or overnight would be better.

When ready to grill, drain excess sauce and reserve. Place chicken on prepared grill, skin side up, about 8-inches from heat. Grill, turning a few times, for about 20 minutes or until fork can be inserted with ease. Brush generously with reserved sauce during 20 minutes of grilling. When chicken is done, place on platter; top with remaining sauce and sprinkle with cheese, if you like.

Sauce method:
In small saucepan make sauce by mixing together onion, tomato sauce, taco sauce, molasses, vinegar, oil, salt, oregano and pepper. Bring mixture to a boil. Remove from heat and cool 2 minutes.

Chicken in a Tex-Mex barbecue sauce — you'll say Olé! I think that means OOH it's so GOOD!!™

Oven-Fried Chicken with Honey Butter Sauce

1 (2½-3 lb.)	broiler, cut up for frying
1 cup	flour
2 tsp.	salt
¼ tsp.	pepper
2 tsp.	paprika
¼ lb.	or ½ cup butter

mix together to make honey butter sauce

¼ cup	melted butter
¼ cup	honey
¼ cup	lemon juice

Dip chicken pieces into mixture of flour, salt, pepper and paprika. Melt butter in a shallow baking pan in a hot oven. Remove baking pan from oven. As pieces of floured chicken are placed in pan, turn, coat with butter, then bake, skin side down, in a single layer. Bake at 400° F., for 30 minutes. Turn chicken. Pour honey butter sauce over chicken. Bake 30 minutes, or until tender. Spoon honey butter sauce over chicken again.

Honey butter sauce:
Melt butter and beat in honey and lemon juice.

Pure Southern hospitality on a platter! Try this once — and you'll be using it as a kitchen standard from then on!

Fancy Fast Chicken

makes 6 servings

3	chicken breasts split, boned, and skinned (that'll give 6 pieces)
6	slices Swiss cheese
¼ lb.	sliced mushrooms (optional)
1 (10¾ oz.) can	cream of chicken soup
½ cup	white wine
2 cups	Pepperidge Farm Herb Stuffing (a small package will do)
1	stick of butter

Place chicken in lightly greased 9 × 13″ glass baking dish. Top each piece with slice of Swiss cheese. If using sliced mushrooms, lay them over the Swiss cheese. Mix can of soup with wine and pour over chicken. Spread stuffing mix over top, and drizzle melted butter over the top. Bake for one hour at 350°. (I have found that with boneless chicken breasts you can bake them for about 45-50 minutes.) OOH it's so GOOD!!™

Last minute company coming? Fancy fast chicken is just the answer! There's crunch, there's richness, there's elegance and it's so darn easy to serve.

Easy Chicken Fricassee   *makes 8 servings*

2	large onions, chopped
4 Tbsp.	oil (or 2 oil and 2 margarine)
4 lbs.	chicken wings separated at the joints
2	cans of mushroom sauce (or from 2 packets)
1 tsp.	paprika
1 tsp.	sugar
½ tsp.	garlic powder
½ tsp.	salt
½ tsp.	pepper
	Rolled into little balls:
3 lbs.	ground beef mixed with
2	eggs
1 cup	bread crumbs
1 tsp.	onion powder
	touch of salt and pepper

In a large saucepan, sauté chopped onions in oil until soft; add disjointed chicken wings until golden. Add sauce and seasonings and cook on medium heat 20 minutes. Add the meatballs and cook 20 minutes more. Adjust seasonings to taste and enjoy. By the way, it tastes better the second day. OOH it's so GOOD!!™

NOTE: I double this amount of sauce because I like it with more gravy.

It's going to taste old fashioned but it's a lot easier! If you want it a little juicier, just add more water. But add a little seasoning, too.

Danish Chicken Breasts   *makes 10 servings*

10	half breasts of chicken, boned (skinned if you wish)
10	strips of Danish natural cream cheese with herbs and spices, ½″ thick, 3″ long
2	eggs, lightly beaten
¼ tsp.	salt
2 cups	fine, soft bread crumbs
4 Tbsp.	oil
2 Tbsp.	butter or margarine

Tuck a strip of cream cheese beneath a raised side of the skin on a boneless breast of chicken (or make a pocket with a sharp knife into the flesh itself, if the breast is skinless). In bowl, blend eggs and salt, dip chicken into egg, then coat with crumbs. Heat oil and butter in skillet. Brown chicken briefly on skin side (1 minute), then on second side (another minute). Transfer to baking pan, cheese side down. Bake in 350° oven, 30-40 minutes. Meat will be succulent and juicy! Serve at once.

Variation:
Using chicken breasts with skin and bone. Loosen skin enough to tuck thin strips of cream cheese under it. Proceed as directed above, coating with egg and bread crumbs. Bake 25 minutes.

Running out of ways to serve chicken?? Here's a new one that's quick, easy and delicious!

Chicken With Orange

8	boneless chicken breast sides (that's 4 whole breasts boned)
1 cup	white wine
1 cup	bottled duck sauce
½ cup	soy sauce
¼ tsp.	garlic powder
1½ cups	corn starch (approx.) vegetable oil for frying juice of ½ orange or
2 Tbsp.	water

Mix together in glass bowl the white wine, bottled duck sauce, soy sauce and garlic powder (reconstitute with a tablespoon of water) for marinade. Cut chicken breasts into large finger size pieces and marinate in the bowl of marinade for a minimum of 15 minutes (up to an hour is ok, too.) Take the chicken fingers out of marinade, shaking them dry, and roll them in a glass dish of corn starch and lay them out on a cookie sheet or a sheet of waxpaper or foil. Heat a skillet to medium with half a cup of vegetable oil and stir fry quickly (moving them around quite often) a handful of chicken breast fingers at a time until they are golden. (Shouldn't be any more than 4 or 5 minutes.) Add more oil as is needed when frying. Remove them by batch and drain them on paper towels laid out on a cookie sheet — When all batches are done, thicken marinade in a saucepan with a tablespoon of the dipping corn starch mixed with two tablespoons of orange juice or water over medium heat. (Don't forget to keep stirring it while it's cooking.)

Serve the chicken fingers on a bed of sliced seedless peeled oranges and drizzle the thickened marinade over them.

Here's a way to combine chicken breasts with some of the abundant navel oranges that are around for a rage oriental marinated dish! I sometimes garnish them with a couple of maraschino cherries and a chopped green onion — boy does it look great!

Skillet Turkey Wings in Barbecue Sauce

makes 2 servings

2	turkey wings, separated at joints
2 Tbsp.	flour
2 Tbsp.	oil
½ cup	chopped onion
1	clove garlic, finely chopped
1 (8 oz.) can	tomato sauce
¼ cup	vinegar
1 Tbsp.	each packed brown sugar and lemon juice
2 tsp.	chili powder
1 tsp.	Worcestershire sauce
⅛ tsp.	each salt and cayenne pepper

Dust turkey with flour. Heat oil in large skillet. Sauté wings 5 to 7 minutes or until lightly browned on all sides. Remove from skillet; set aside. Add onion and garlic to skillet; cook until onion is tender. Stir in tomato sauce, vinegar, sugar, lemon juice, chili powder, Worcestershire, salt and cayenne until well blended. Return wings to skillet. Baste with sauce; cover and simmer 1 hour or until tender.

Who cares if it rains — all year long I've got barbecued turkey wings. Make it a little warmer and really Tex-Mex tasting with a little more cayenne and/or hot pepper sauce.

Easy Turkey Pot Pie

2 cups	cooked, cubed turkey
1 (10¾ oz.) can	cream of celery soup, undiluted
2 (15 oz.) cans	mixed vegetables, drained
1½ cups	chicken or turkey stock
1 stick	margarine or butter, melted
1½ cups	biscuit baking mix
1½ cups	milk

Mix together turkey pieces, soup, mixed vegetables and stock. Set aside. Coat a 13 × 9″ casserole with the melted margarine. Pour out excess margarine and reserve for later use. Next, pour vegetable-turkey mixture into the buttered casserole dish. Blend together the biscuit baking mix, milk and excess margarine. Blend until almost smooth. Pour topping mixture over vegetable and turkey mixture.

Bake pie in a 350° F. oven for 1 hour. OOH it's so GOOD!!™

This is the easiest way to make pot pie — just throw the top in and let it bake itself on — You'll look like you learned how to make this while on a grandma's knee (but it's a lot easier than hers was).

Turkey Oscar*

makes 6 to 8 servings

6	turkey cutlets, sliced about ⅓" thick
2	eggs
2 Tbsp.	water
1 cup	bread crumbs (approx.)
½ cup	salad oil
1	package Bearnaisse or Hollandaise sauce
1 can	asparagus spears or
1 lb.	trimmed and cooked fresh asparagus or
1 pkg.	frozen asparagus
1 can	flaked crabmeat or
½ lb.	imitation crabmeat

Beat the egg and water together. Heat the salad oil in skillet. Dip the turkey slices in the egg mixture, and then in the bread crumbs. Sauté in the hot oil. Add salt and pepper to taste. While the turkey slices are sauteeing, prepare the Bearnaisse or Hollandaise sauce according to package directions. When the turkey is all sauteed, place the slices in a baking pan, whether microwave or one that is for the conventional oven. Place the asparagus spears on top of the turkey. Place the crabmeat on top of the asparagus, and spoon the sauce on top of the crabmeat. Place dish in the microwave for approximately 4 minutes, turning after two minutes. If using conventional oven, preheat to 375° and place baking pan in oven for approximately 20 minutes until sauce is bubbling. OOH it's so GOOD!!™

*From the North Carolina Turkey Cooking Contest

This sounds so fancy, looks so fancy, tastes so fancy — but it doesn't cost fancy or take fancy work.

BEEF, VEAL, LAMB & PORK

You bet!!

These are still the mainstay of the main courses of our tables.

The meat industry is doing just so many things to fit today's standards of leaner and easier that it will always be our favorite for wanting to "sink our teeth into."

These recipes I've picked for this section are the favorites for tastes — old fashioned taste along with the ease of making it in the modern way, quick, easy, and sensible — and so many of them can be made beforehand at our convenience, and then rewarmed when we need them. (Most of them taste better when they're rewarmed, also.)

Now, doesn't all this make sense — you bet!!

Sweet and Sour Beef Brisket

6 to 7 lbs.	beef brisket, well trimmed (1st cut also known as single brisket)
1 Tbsp.	salt
½ Tbsp.	pepper
1	clove garlic, minced
1 Tbsp.	paprika
⅓ cup	brown sugar
2 Tbsp.	vinegar
½ cup	catsup
1	onion, sliced

Season brisket with salt, pepper, garlic and paprika. Put brisket in a roasting pan. Mix sugar, vinegar and catsup and pour over the top. Spread onion slices on top and cover roaster with foil. Place in 350° oven and cook for 2½ to 3 hours. Remove from oven and let cool. Place in refrigerator and let the whole brisket sit there until the day you intend to serve it (it can sit happily for a week to 10 days). On the serving day, remove brisket from the juices and slice it thinly and diagonally. Return meat slices to pan juices, recover with foil and place in a 350° oven for 45 minutes. You may serve from the pan, if it is halfway decent looking, or spread the meat slices on a platter and drizzle the juices over the top.

Yes, this can be made at your convenience a good 9 or 10 days ahead so you don't have to rush at the last minute. And the longer it stays up to that 10 days, the better it gets. I love it! It's no fail.

Oriental Pot Roast

makes 8 to 12 servings

1 (2 to 3 lb.)	beef chuck pot roast
⅓ cup	cooking oil
⅓ cup	soy sauce
2 Tbsp.	lemon juice
2 Tbsp.	honey
1	clove garlic, minced
1¼ tsp.	ground ginger
2 cups	celery bias sliced into ½ inch pieces
4	medium carrots, bias sliced into ½ inch pieces (1½ cups)
2	medium onions, quartered
¼ cup	cold water
1 Tbsp.	cornstarch

Trim excess fat from meat. Place meat in a plastic bag. Set in a deep bowl. For marinade, combine cooking oil, soy sauce, lemon juice, honey, garlic, and ginger. Pour over meat; close bag. Marinate overnight in refrigerator. Turn bag occasionally to distribute marinade.

Next day, transfer roast and marinade from bag to 4 quart Dutch oven. Cover; simmer for an hour. Add celery, carrots, and onions. Cover and simmer about 1 hour and 45 minutes more or until meat and vegetables are tender. Remove meat and vegetables to a heated platter to keep warm.

For gravy, skim excess fat from pan juices. Pour juices into 2-cup measure. Add water to juices if necessary to make 1¼ cups liquid; return to Dutch Oven. Combine the ¼ cup cold water and cornstarch; add to pan juices. Cook and stir till thickened and bubbly. Serve gravy with meat and vegetables. (Optional: if you like a thicker gravy.)

Anybody can do it — It's one of my standards and company favorites. It may take a little longer cooking time than the recipe calls for. Try adding pineapple chunks for a sweet sour taste once in a while. A one-dish meal that saves a mess to clean up.

Italian Beef Stew with Rosemary

makes 4 servings

1½ lbs.	boneless beef chuck, cut in 1 inch cubes
3 Tbsp.	oil
1	large onion, chopped
⅔ cup	diced celery
2	cloves garlic, divided
1 (28 oz.) can	tomatoes, preferably Italian, cut up
½ cup	minced parsley
½ cup	dry white wine
1½ tsp.	salt
1 tsp.	rosemary
½ tsp.	pepper

In large heavy saucepan, brown beef in hot oil. Remove and set aside. Add onion, celery and garlic to pan drippings; Sauté until tender. Return beef to pan. Add tomatoes, parsley, wine, salt, rosemary and pepper. Bring to boil; reduce heat, cover and simmer 1½ to 2 hours or until beef is tender.

The rosemary adds a whole new authentic Italian Mediterranean taste. Nobody'll know exactly what that exciting taste is. Use chili powder and call it a Mexican Holiday stew every so often.

Ungarische Gulasch (Hungarian Goulash)

makes 5 servings

2 lbs.	beef chuck, rump or round
1	onion, large, finely chopped
2 Tbsp.	lard or shortening
¼ cup	sweet Hungarian paprika
¼ cup	flour
1½ tsp.	salt
1 cup	water, boiling

Cut meat into 1½ inch cubes, removing excess fat and gristle. Cook onion in lard until yellow and transparent; do not brown. Add paprika; blend. Add flour, salt, and water; cook and stir until thickened. Add meat; cover. Simmer gently only until tender, about 1½ hours, adding a little water from time to time if needed. Serve with boiled potatoes or noodles.

Super easy goulash — serve it over cooked wide noodles with buttered rye bread.

Chunky Chili

2 Tbsp.	vegetable oil
1	medium onion, chopped
1½ lbs.	chunk beef (cut into ¾″ pieces)
1 (3 oz.) can	tomato paste
1 can	whole tomatoes
¾ tsp.	garlic powder
2 Tbsp.	chili powder
1 tsp.	oregano
1 can	kidney beans, drained

When oil sputters in skillet, sauté onion. Add beef and brown. Pour off drippings. Then add tomato paste, whole tomatoes, chili and garlic powders and oregano. Simmer about 1 hour, stirring frequently. Stir in kidney beans and simmer 30 minutes longer until meat is fork tender. If mixture is dry, add small quantity of water.

Everyone has a recipe for chili but here's one that you can vary to suit your own taste and it's easy besides.

Spicy Chili

¾ lb.	ground beef
¼ cup	chopped green pepper
¼ cup	chopped onion
1 (16 oz.) can	tomatoes, whole or peeled
1 (16 oz.) can	tomato sauce
1 (16 oz.) can	red kidney beans
½ tsp.	oregano
¼ tsp.	garlic powder
2 tsp.	chili powder
¼ tsp.	salt
½ tsp.	basil
¼ tsp.	pepper
	Hot cooked rice or corn bread squares

Brown beef slowly in a skillet. Add green pepper and onion and simmer over low heat until onion becomes transparent. Drain off excess fat. Stir in tomatoes, tomato sauce, undrained kidney beans, chili powder, salt, basil, oregano, garlic powder and pepper. Bring to a boil and reduce heat. Cover and simmer 20 minutes. Serve in bowls over cooked rice or serve with corn bread.

A delicious variety of chili that you can make in minutes rather than hours, but tastes like you made the hours' version.

Picadillo

1½ lbs.	ground beef, brown with a large minced onion in 3 Tbsp. of cooking oil. Then add and mix in:
1 lb. can	tomatoes (undrained)
½ cup	chopped stuffed olives
½ cup	seedless raisins (Plump them up in warm water first. It's better that way.)
¼ tsp.	garlic powder
	salt and pepper to taste

I put in a diced green pepper, a tsp. of chili powder, an ⅛ tsp. of cinnamon and a shake of cayenne pepper also. Super. Serve over rice.

Nice Tex-Mex version of a sloppy joe. The raisins make it a sweet and sour version of a Tex-Mex or a Caribbean Sloppy Joe. Leave them in or leave them out.

Steak Teriyaki

1	beef tip sirloin cut to 1¼" thick (you may use other tender beef steaks such as top loin, t-bone, porterhouse, and rib eye steaks)
½ cup	soy sauce
¼ cup	brown sugar
1 tsp.	ground ginger
1	clove garlic, minced

Combine soy sauce, brown sugar, ginger and garlic. Place steak on grill. When first side is browned, brush with teriyaki sauce, turn and finish cooking the second side, brushing with sauce occasionally. Carve the steak across grain into thin slices.

Brush the sauce on your favorite steak or hamburger or chicken — teriyaki gives you a delicious coating without losing the taste of the meat itself!

Reuben Meatloaf

makes 6 to 8 servings

2 lbs.	ground beef
2 cups	soft bread crumbs
1	egg, slightly beaten
2 Tbsp.	catsup
¾ tsp.	salt
1 (8 oz.) can	sauerkraut, rinsed and drained
1 cup	shredded Swiss cheese
¼ lb.	pastrami, chopped
¼ cup	dairy sour cream
1 Tbsp.	French's America's Favorite Yellow Mustard

Combine ground beef, bread crumbs, egg, catsup and salt in bowl, mixing lightly. Combine sauerkraut, ¾ cup of the Swiss cheese, pastrami, sour cream and mustard. Pat out one third of meat mixture to form an oval 9 inches long on oven-proof platter or baking dish. Then spread with one half of the sauerkraut mixture. Repeat layers of meat and sauerkraut mixture. Use remaining one third of meat mixture for top layer of loaf. Bake at 350° for 60 minutes, loosely covered with foil tent. Remove tent. Sprinkle remaining cheese on top of loaf and bake 5 more minutes.

Microwave: prepare meatloaf and filling as directed. Layer in 10-inch glass pie pan with custard cup placed in center. Cover loosely with wax paper and microwave on high 10 to 12 minutes or until meatloaf is cooked. Uncover; pour off pan juices. Sprinkle with remaining ¼ cup cheese and microwave, uncovered, on high 1 minute. OOH it's so GOOD!!™

A meatloaf that tastes like a Reuben sandwich — you'll think you're eating in a deli!

Easy Stuffed Peppers

1	large onion, finely chopped
2 Tbsp.	oil
1 lb.	finely chopped brown and serve sausage
½ cup	seasoned bread crumbs
1 cup	grated cheese (such as cheddar or Swiss)
1	well beaten egg
4	green or red peppers, halved, cleaned and blanched for 4-5 minutes

Sauté onion in oil until just starting to soften. Add sausage until warm and remove from stove. Add to warm skillet and mix well bread crumbs, cheese and egg. Stuff mixture into peppers cut lengthwise. Put into a baking dish and then into a preheated 350° oven for 20 to 25 minutes. Enjoy.

Options to put into mixture before cooking: ¼ cup catsup, 1 teaspoon oregano or chili powder or mint leaves, or tarragon or thyme or whatever makes you happy. A ¼ teaspoon of cayenne will heat it up also.

*Everyone has a stuffed pepper recipe —
but here's a twist that will give you a little
different taste so you can serve them
again without being boring! Make it your
own by adding oregano, or cayenne, or
pepper, or mint leaves or even chili
powder for that Tex-Mex flavor!*

Basic Meat Stuffing

1 lb.	ground beef
3 Tbsp.	uncooked rice
1	egg
¼ cup	chopped onion
1 tsp.	salt
¼ cup	catsup
¼ tsp.	pepper
1 Tbsp.	water
1 Tbsp.	steak sauce (like French's or A-1)

Mix well. Put in whatever other seasonings you might want (if any), and use to stuff cabbage, peppers or onions.

Try your own favorite seasonings to please the family! If you like stuffed cabbage and stuffed peppers — try this next time in onions — that's right — onions — you'll love it!

Danish Meatballs (Frikadeller) *makes about 3 dozen*

1 lb.	ground beef mixed with 1 lb. ground veal or ground pork
1 Tbsp.	salt
1 tsp.	pepper
¾ cup	flour
1	medium onion, grated
2	eggs
1½ cups	water
	butter for frying

In bowl, combine all ingredients, except butter, blending thoroughly. Let stand 15 minutes to allow flour to absorb water. Heat butter in skillet until very hot. Shape meatballs with metal tablespoon, first dipped in hot butter. (You can use a teaspoon to get cocktail size for passing around at a party.) Fry on medium heat about 5 minutes per side.

One of my all time favorite recipes! It's a simple party time hors d'oeuvre!

Glazed Meatballs*

makes 65

3	slices bread
⅔ cup	milk
2	slightly beaten eggs
1 Tbsp.	prepared horseradish
1½ lbs.	ground beef
½ cup	catsup
¼ cup	maple-flavored syrup
¼ cup	soy sauce
1 tsp.	ground allspice
½ tsp.	dry mustard

Soak bread in milk until soft. Stir in eggs, horseradish, 1 teaspoon salt, and ¼ teaspoon pepper. Add beef; mix well. Shape into ¾-inch meatballs; place on rack in shallow baking pan. Bake in 450° oven 10 to 15 minutes. Remove from pan; cool. Arrange meatballs in single layer on baking sheet so edges do not touch. Freeze till firm. Wrap in moisture-vaporproof wrap; freeze till ready to heat.

Before serving, in saucepan combine catsup, maple-flavored syrup, soy sauce, allspice, mustard, and ¼ cup water. Stir in frozen meatballs. Heat to boiling; stirring often. Reduce heat; keep warm. Serve in chafing dish. Serve with wooden picks.

*From *Better Homes and Gardens*

> *Be ready for that holiday or unexpected company — keep a batch in your freezer. Just toothpicks and napkins make it an instant party!*

Hickory Smoked Barbecue Ribs
makes 8 servings

4 to 5 lbs.	pork ribs (spareribs or backribs)
1 (3½ oz.) bottle	Wright's Hickory Liquid Smoke
2½ quarts	water
1 bottle	of your favorite barbecue sauce

Combine liquid smoke and water in a large pot. Bring to boil; add the ribs and reduce heat and simmer 1½ to 2 hours. Use exhaust fan to eliminate cooking odor. Remove ribs from liquid, cool. Ribs may be refrigerated or frozen for future use. Dip or brush ribs with barbecue sauce. Place in a 400° oven for 15 to 20 minutes. For crusty ribs, broil for 3 to 5 minutes.

Ribs may be prepared in a browning bag. Place ribs in a single layer in a large size oven cooking bag in a baking pan. Add 1 bottle of smoke and 1 quart water. Close bag with tie and with a fork make 4 small holes in the top. Bake in a 325° oven for 1½ hours.

For parties, have your butcher trim ribs to cocktail size. 4 pounds will serve 10 to 12.

I cut the liquid smoke by a half and it's just like southern, real southern ribs — but in a shortcut style.

Lamb Ka-Bob
makes 30-35 medium size ka-bobs

5 lbs.	ground lamb
1 cup	chopped fresh parsley
1½ cups	finely chopped onion (almost grated)
	salt and pepper
½ cup	tomato sauce

Mix together and shape onto pointed skewers. Broil in oven or on grill to desired doneness. OOH it's so GOOD!!™

Lamb sounds exotic — but it's really versatile! Tired of grilling the same old things — Lamb-Ka-Bobs are just the answer!

Garlic Braised Lamb Shanks

12	American lamb shanks
⅓ cup	salad oil
½ cup	flour seasoned with:
1½ tsp.	thyme
1 Tbsp.	paprika
1 tsp.	salt
½ tsp.	rosemary
4-5-6	cloves of garlic, minced, or good ½ tsp. granulated garlic
1 cup	finely chopped onion (optional) (I use them)
3 cups	chicken or beef broth or stock or even water will do

Dredge the lamb shanks in the seasoned flour and brown them in a pan with ⅓ cup salad oil. Sprinkle the rest of the flour mixture and the garlic on the shanks, put in 3 cups of broth, stock or water (and onions if you choose) and braise in a 325° to 350° oven for 1½ hours. Remove from oven and cool to skim off the fat that rises to the top. Cook for 2 more hours and serve. However, I like to cool it, refrigerate it, and the next day remove the solidified fat. Reheat it for another hour; it seems to be richer and yet leaner. Enjoy.

This is so easy for so much taste. The color is such a nice brown that it looks like it's old-fashioned pot roasted crisp. Serve with mashed potatoes so you can use up all the gravy.

Veal Scallopini

2 lbs.	veal cutlets (pounded to about ¼″ and cut into medallions)
1 tsp.	salt
⅛ tsp.	pepper
1 cup	Marsala or sherry wine
½ cup	flour
1 cup	chicken or beef broth
½	lemon
1 tsp.	oregano

Sprinkle the veal with salt and pepper and place in glass bowl. Pour over medallions the Marsala or sherry wine. Marinate covered in refrigerator for 1 hour (1½ hours at most). Drain the medallions, reserving the wine. Dip medallions in flour and brown them in a stick of butter in large skillet. When browned add chicken or beef broth, juice of ½ lemon, the reserved wine, and oregano. Simmer for 8 to 10 minutes (stir the sauce every so often while cooking).

Try adding sliced mushrooms or canned tomatoes along with a few seasonings if you'd like — With this version of the Italian classic, you'll say OOH it's so GOOD!!™ — And that means it's got to be Italian.

POTATOES & RICE

So many of us look forward to the potato (or rice) — (or pasta) on our plates as much as we do anything else. I know I do — the mail requests certainly support that. Well, here are the ones most requested.

Here's where you can really be creative.

You can zig and zag with your spice rack, your leftovers, your presentation, your garnishing, and your family taste favorites, without ever disturbing your pocketbook — Oh!! How nice!!

German Potato Salad

5 lbs.	boiled potatoes, cold, sliced
½ cup	corn oil
½ cup	white vinegar
¼ cup	sugar
1 tsp.	salt
	Parsley, chopped fine as needed

Mix dressing ingredients together. Stir in potatoes. Refrigerate for two hours before serving.

> *The Basic German Potato Salad. From here you can add bacon bits, ham cubes, dill, any and/or all of these.*

Dill New Potato Salad

10 lbs.	cooked new potatoes, quartered
2 cups	sour cream
6 Tbsp.	dill weed
1 tsp.	salt
1 tsp.	pepper
1½ cups	chopped scallions
4 tsp.	chopped garlic
	dash Worcestershire sauce
	dash Tabasco

Combine all ingredients and mix with warm potatoes. Chill and serve garnished with fresh dill and scallion slices. We suggest you leave the red skins on the potatoes for color and texture.

> *This works nice with the little new potatoes too (red or white). Just don't quarter them. Serve it warm or cold.*

Down Home Potatoes
makes 6 servings

Boil 2 lbs. of peeled potatoes until almost tender. Slice them about ¼" thick. Layer them into a well buttered 9 × 13 inch baking dish (glass). Moisten each layer with 3 or 4 tablespoons of heavy cream (and a teaspoon of finely chopped onion, if you like.) And lightly sprinkle garlic powder, paprika, salt and pepper, and a handful of grated cheese. It'll take only 2 layers, or 3 at most. Bake that in a 350° oven for about an hour — 'til it's golden.
Enjoy! OOH it's so GOOD!!™

> *I like to use a heavier hand with the herbs and grated cheese. Variables include the onions, different spices and herbs, different cheeses. Have fun!*

Parmesan Potato Sticks
makes 6 servings

2 lbs.	Washington russet potatoes
½ cup	butter or margarine, melted
½ cup	fine dry bread crumbs
½ cup	grated parmesan cheese
½ tsp.	salt
⅛ tsp.	garlic powder
⅛ tsp.	pepper

Peel potatoes and cut lengthwise into quarters. Cut each quarter into 3 strips. Roll in melted butter, then in mixture of crumbs, cheese, salt, garlic powder and pepper. Place in single layer in shallow baking dish. Pour any remaining melted butter over potatoes. Bake at 400°, 30 to 35 minutes, until potatoes are tender. OOH it's so GOOD!!™

> *Here's a dandy change from every day French fries! They'll be tender on the inside and cheese tasting crisp on the outside!*

Striped Spuds

makes 4-6 servings

4	large potatoes
¼ cup	butter or margarine, melted
2 Tbsp.	French's Bold 'N Spicy Deli Mustard
1 tsp.	sugar
½ tsp.	French's seasoning salt
½ tsp.	French's Italian seasoning

Cook potatoes in boiling salted water until just tender, 20 to 25 minutes. Meanwhile, combine remaining ingredients for basting sauce. Peel potatoes, if desired, and cut into ¾-inch thick slices. Brush generously with sauce. Grill over hot coals until deep golden brown on both sides.

> *We do our meats, poultry, even fish on the grill — so why not a potato, also!*

Baked Mashed Potatoes

makes 4-6 servings

4 cups	mashed potatoes, at room temperature
1 (8 oz.) pkg.	cream cheese, softened
1	egg
¾ cup	finely chopped onion

Preheat oven to 350° F. Lightly grease a 2-quart casserole; set aside. Combine potatoes, cream cheese, and egg in a large bowl; beat with electric mixer until smooth. Stir in onion. Spoon into prepared casserole. Bake 1 hour. Serve hot, sprinkled with chopped parsley or scallions.

> *You can't go wrong with an old standby — try this old favorite with some chopped parsley or maybe scallions!*

Smart Au Gratin Potatoes *makes 10-12 servings*

2 lbs.	frozen hash browns or 6 cups fresh, raw hash brown potatoes
2 cups	grated cheddar or colby cheese
1 cup	finely chopped onion
1 (8 oz.) pkg.	sour cream
1	can cream of mushroom soup
	butter
	crushed potato chips or bacon bits
½ tsp.	salt

In a large bowl, mix mushroom soup, sour cream, cheese, salt and onions. Then add hash browns. (If you are using frozen hash browns, let them thaw a bit before adding to mixture.) Mix well. Pour into a $9 \times 13''$ cake pan, dot with butter, then top with potato chips or bacon bits. Bake at 350° for 35-45 minutes. Also parsley flakes or garlic salt added to mixture makes for a delightfully different taste.

A downhome favorite made in a smart shortcut style that takes all the work out and leaves in all the taste!

Crisp Potato Skins

6	medium potatoes (about 2 lbs.)
¼ cup	melted butter or margarine
1 tsp.	soy sauce

Preheat oven to 400° F. Scrub potatoes thoroughly and pierce each with a fork. Bake until potatoes are tender, about 45 minutes to 1 hour. Cook, then cut in quarters lengthwise and then in half crosswise to form 8 sections. Scoop flesh from skins leaving ⅛-inch shell. Reserve flesh for use in another recipe.

Increase oven temperature to 500° F. Mix together melted butter and soy sauce and brush on both sides of skins. Place skins on baking sheet and bake until crisp, about 10 to 12 minutes.

These can be made ahead and reheated in 400° F. oven for about 8 minutes. Serve sprinkled with coarse salt and top as desired.

NOTE: Uses for scooped potato pulp: 1) Mash and season. Add your choice of chopped green pepper and tomato, sliced green onions or shredded cheese. Reheat in a casserole for tomorrow night's dinner. 2) Add sautéed onion to potato. Use to fill an omelet. 3) Make a mashed potato salad using your favorite dressing. 4) Mash and stir into soups to thicken. 5) Season to taste and form into patties. Dust with flour and sauté in butter until browned on both sides.

From the Potato Board.

Potato skins are the rage — here's one of the show's favorites!

Swiss Skillet Potato Cake *makes 4 servings*

1 lb.	new potatoes, cooked, pared
2 Tbsp.	finely chopped chives or scallions
½ tsp.	salt
3	eggs, lightly beaten
¼ cup	light or heavy cream
¼ cup	parmesan cheese, grated
½ cup	Swiss cheese, grated
½ tsp.	salt
½ tsp.	pepper
¼ cup	butter
3 Tbsp.	parsley, chopped

Shred potatoes; add salt and chives. Mix eggs, cream, cheeses, salt and pepper. Heat butter in 10″ skillet over medium heat. Add potatoes to cover bottom evenly. Pour egg mixture over it; cook for about 20 minutes or until potatoes are brown. Invert potato cakes in skillet; cook for about 10 minutes. Remove to round dish; cut into wedges. Garnish with chopped parsley; serve hot. OOH it's so GOOD!!™

From *Restaurants & Institutions*

This is the Swiss version of a potato pancake! But nicely different from a potato pancake!

Rosemary Potatoes

⅓ cup	olive oil
1½ tsp.	salt
½ tsp.	freshly ground black pepper
1½ tsp.	rosemary leaves (ground rosemary would not be suitable for use in this recipe; use only the leaves)
3 lbs.	potatoes

In a very large bowl, combine olive oil, salt, and pepper. Gently crush the rosemary with mortar and pestle. Blend into the olive oil. Preheat the oven to 350°. Scrub the potatoes very well and slice very thin. Toss in the olive oil until thoroughly coated. Divide the potatoes between two large shallow baking dishes. Bake, uncovered, in preheated oven until potatoes are tender but still firm, approximately 1 hour and 15 minutes.

Tastes fresh from a French country kitchen.

Home Fried Fresh Yams
makes 4 servings

4 cups	pared fresh North Carolina yams sliced ¼" thick (approx. 4 large yams)
6 Tbsp.	salad oil
1 tsp.	salt

Cover sliced, peeled yams with cold water. Drain on paper towel. Heat oil in skillet and place potatoes in pan. Fry 10-15 minutes turning frequently until brown and crisp. Season with salt. OOH it's so GOOD!!™

Here's an old standard with a new twist!

Cajun Rice

1 (9 oz.) box	rice pilaf or 6 cups of cooked rice
1 cup	chopped onion
½	green or red pepper, chopped
¼ lb.	chopped mushrooms
¼ lb.	diced chicken liver
½ lb.	diced sausage (like Kielbasa or hot dogs, etc.)
1 Tbsp.	Worcestershire sauce
½ tsp.	garlic powder
½ tsp.	hot pepper sauce (salt and pepper if needed)

Prepare rice pilaf according to package directions. Mix all other ingredients in skillet and sauté until soft. Mix skillet ingredients into pilaf or rice and enjoy. Add chopped parsley or chopped green onions for color. And don't be afraid to add your own favorite seasonings if you wish. It'll work fine. And OOH it's so GOOD!!™

A hearty old-fashioned tasting rice dish in a snap. This shows perfectly the adaptability and creativity of being able to use inexpensive, easy-to-get items!

Shrimp Fried Rice

2 cups	chopped cooked shrimp
2 Tbsp.	soy sauce
4 cups	boiled rice
¼ cup	oil
2	eggs, lightly beaten
1 (4 oz.) can	mushrooms (drained)
1 tsp.	salt
	freshly ground black pepper
½ cup	scallions, chopped

Fry shrimp in oil in deep frying pan for 1 minute, stirring constantly. Add eggs, mushrooms, salt and pepper, and fry over medium heat for 5 minutes, stirring constantly. Add rice and soy sauce and fry for 5 minutes, stirring frequently. Mix with chopped scallions. OOH it's so GOOD!!™

> *It's a whole meal or a side dish! Just like you'll find in your favorite Chinese restaurant! Try it with imitation crab meat, beef, chicken, or pork, or maybe mushrooms! You decide!*

Regal Rice and Asparagus   *makes 8 servings*

2 lbs.	fresh asparagus, cleaned, trimmed and cut into 1″ pieces
2 cups	rice, cooked and cooled
¼ tsp.	salt
¼ tsp.	ground red pepper
⅓ cup	sour cream
⅔ cup	milk
½ lb.	sharp cheddar cheese, grated

Cook asparagus in boiling water for 10 minutes until tender-crisp. Combine rice, salt, pepper, sour cream, milk and one half of cheese. Spoon half of rice mixture into 1 greased pan (9×9″). Arrange asparagus on top and spread remaining rice mixture over asparagus. Bake at 350° for 25 minutes. Sprinkle remaining cheese over top of casserole during the last five minutes of baking or after removal from oven. OOH it's so GOOD!!™

> *Something a little different you can do with asparagus — the "regal" vegetable.*

VEGGIES

We used to be restricted to rigid seasons for enjoying vegetables — now we can have almost any of them almost all year long, almost like from our backyard, almost at local prices. They're coming in from someplace in the world that they're growing at almost our whim.

And with all the technology in agriculture, we're going to be even more pampered in the very near future — and the future is certainly veggies — crunchy, fresh, easy, quick, versatile, healthy, economical. All of those and more.

I told you — the future is deliciously now!!

And these recipes can help you in all those ways — they're the most requested so they've gotta be yummie.

Not Fried Eggplant

No spattering, no frying pan to clean, no last minute burning, because it's fried in the oven.

Slice a medium to large size eggplant into ½ inch slices, then those into inch by 4 inch strips

Toss the strips in ½ cup of oil and then into a mixture of ¾ cup of seasoned bread crumbs and ¼ cup parmesan or romano cheese, then add

¼ tsp.   salt
⅛ tsp.   pepper

Put them on a foil lined cookie sheet and bake them in a preheated 375° oven for about 15 to 20 minutes. And they come out golden and crisp – Enjoy!

I like mine with sour cream and chives. OOH it's so GOOD!!™

I cook these a lot longer than 20 minutes to get them crisp. I don't know where I ever got the idea that 20 minutes was enough. Great side dish or appetizer. As an appetizer, the sour cream and chives are served as a dip.

Baked Eggplant with Cheese Italian Style

6	small eggplants, sliced in ½" rounds
1	egg, beaten
1 cup	bread crumbs
2 Tbsp.	vegetable oil
	salt and pepper to taste
1 Tbsp.	parsley or chives
1 (5 oz.) can	sliced mushrooms, drained
1 (15 oz.) can	tomato sauce
6	thin slices tomato
8	slices mozzarella cheese
1 tsp.	grated onion

Dip eggplant slices in egg and then in bread crumbs. Heat vegetable oil in skillet; brown eggplant lightly on both sides. Arrange in buttered baking dish. Season to taste and sprinkle with parsley or chives and sliced mushrooms. Pour tomato sauce over casserole. Top with tomato slices first and then cheese slices. Sprinkle grated onion over cheese. Bake in a 375°F oven for 30 minutes or until cheese slices are melted. Serve with Italian bread.

This is a fresher version of eggplant parmigiana. Nice for tomato season — and it's always eggplant season.

French Fried Pepper Rings

3-6	sweet green or red peppers (or both) (depending on size)
⅔ cup	milk
½ cup	all purpose flour
1 Tbsp.	cornstarch
¾ tsp.	baking powder
¼ tsp.	salt
	vegetable oil (enough for deep frying in 1″ depth)

Wash peppers, remove stems and seeds. Cut into rings about ⅜″ thick. Heat oil (1 inch deep) in a saucepan (or my favorite an electric fry pan) to 375°. Beat remaining ingredients well with a rotary or electric beater until smooth. Dip each ring into batter letting excess drip into bowl. Fry a few rings at a time till brown. It only takes about 2 minutes. Drain on paper towels and serve. Enjoy.

After eating peppers this way, it spoils you for any other way. Probably one of the all time favorite vegetable recipes I've had on TV. You can use other veggies in this batter too, but, I love these the most.

Crustless Vegetable Pie

makes 5-6 servings

1	small eggplant, peeled and cubed
2	medium zucchini, cubed
1	medium onion, chopped
¼ cup	oil
4	medium tomatoes, peeled and chopped or
1 (#1) can	whole drained tomatoes
3	eggs
¾ cup	parmesan cheese
1 Tbsp.	minced parsley
½ tsp.	basil
½ tsp.	oregano
	salt and pepper
¼ lb.	mozzarella cheese, thinly sliced or shredded

Sauté eggplant, zucchini and onion in oil until vegetables are softened, about 5 to 10 minutes. Add tomatoes, cover and simmer 20-25 minutes, until mixture is soft. (If using canned tomatoes, reduce cooking time to 10 minutes.) Transfer to bowl and cool. Preheat oven to 350°. Beat eggs with ¼ cup parmesan cheese, parsley, basil and oregano. Add to vegetables with salt and pepper to taste. Pour half of mixture into greased (10″) pie pan and top with ¼ cup cheese. Layer with remaining vegetables and cheese. Top with mozzarella and bake 40-45 minutes or until set and cheese is golden brown. OOH it's so GOOD!!™

Great idea for lunch, brunch or a light main dish! This turns your favorite veggies into a crustless pie that spins that wondering of what to serve into a whole bunch of hurrays!

Vegetable Pancakes

Mix together the following:

½ cup	grated parmesan
⅔ cup	flour
1 tsp.	baking powder
8	eggs
2 tsp.	oil
1 tsp.	salt
½ tsp.	pepper
¼ cup	finely chopped onion or finely sliced scallions
4 cups	zucchini or carrots or yams (shredded and lightly pressed) or any chopped cooked vegetable

Adjust mixture to good pancake batter consistency with 2 tablespoons of bread crumbs. Fry as you would pancakes using ½ cup of batter for each. I use a greased electric skillet to maintain a 375°-400° temperature. OOH it's so GOOD!!™

If it needs more bread crumbs, go ahead. This works with almost any chopped veggie.

Orange Glazed Carrots and Parsnips

makes 4 servings

3	medium carrots, sliced diagonally, 1″ thick
3	medium parsnips, sliced diagonally, 1″ thick
2 Tbsp.	freshly squeezed orange juice
2 Tbsp.	honey
1 Tbsp.	butter or margarine
¼ tsp.	freshly grated orange peel

In a medium saucepan, cook carrots and parsnips in one inch of boiling, salted water until almost tender; drain. Add orange juice, honey, butter and orange peel. Cook over medium heat tossing occasionally until vegetables are tender and evenly glazed.

And, if you don't have parsnips, what a nice orange carrot dish. For an easy every season fish or meat accompaniment.

Green Beans with Herbs

1 pkg.	frozen green beans
2 Tbsp.	vegetable oil
1 tsp.	marjoram (or use a tsp. of parsley instead of marjoram if that's handier)
⅛ tsp.	garlic powder
2 Tbsp.	chopped onion
2 Tbsp.	chopped celery

Cook green beans according to package directions (just to tender stage). Combine with remaining ingredients in saucepan. Simmer 5 minutes. Serve hot or chilled.

Use a tsp. of parsley instead of marjoram if that's handier or try your own special seasonings to make it a family favorite! Tastes like spring!

Green Beans Done Just Right

1 lb.	trimmed green beans
5 Tbsp.	butter
	salt and pepper to taste
1 Tbsp.	minced fresh parsley
1	minced garlic clove
	juice of half a lemon

Sauté green beans in butter, along with salt and pepper, minced fresh parsley and minced garlic clove for about 7 minutes, or until just tender. Sprinkle with lemon juice and serve. If there are any left over, chill them and add to salads.

Some people call green beans, pole beans and some call them string beans. Save them and serve them cold in your favorite salad!

Bean Royal

¼ cup	vegetable oil (olive preferred)
1	large minced onion
1 tsp.	basil ⎫
1 tsp.	oregano ⎬ or one Tbsp. of any one
1 tsp.	thyme ⎭
2 tsp.	salt (or less if you wish)
1 tsp.	black pepper
¼ tsp.	cayenne pepper or crushed red pepper
2	shakes hot pepper sauce
¼ tsp.	garlic powder (optional)
1 (16 oz.) can	white beans
1½ cups	water (or more)

Sauté the onion in the oil until very soft. Add the seasonings, white beans and the water and heat thoroughly and boil one minute. Stir a couple of times. You may add more of anything you might like. To make this into "Pasta Fagioli" add a 28 oz. can of tomatoes undrained, ¼ teaspoon of garlic powder and ½ pound of Ditalino or other pasta (cooked and drained). Mix again, warm and adjust seasonings. Serve with crusty bread and grated parmesan for sprinkling. Enjoy!

It's a simple throw together dish! You can use dried beans, but don't forget to soak them first! The fun of this recipe is to try your own favorites in it!

Tomatoes and Onions September Style

½ cup	wine vinegar
⅓ cup	salad oil
1 Tbsp.	dried basil (or ¼ cup chopped fresh basil, if available)
¼ cup	chopped parsley
1 tsp.	dried tarragon (or 1 Tbsp. chopped fresh tarragon, if available)
½ tsp.	oregano
¼ tsp.	black pepper
½ tsp.	garlic powder or a mashed clove of fresh garlic (Both of these are optional)
5-8	tomatoes (depending on size)
1	sweet onion

Mix together for marinade all ingredients except tomatoes and onion. Slice thin the tomatoes and layer half of the slices in a bowl, sprinkle them with a teaspoon of sugar, wet that down with half of the liquid mixture. Layer on a thinly sliced sweet onion, then layer on the rest of the tomatoes. Sprinkle them with another tablespoon of sugar. Then pour on the rest of the liquid. Cover, chill in the refrigerator for a couple of hours. And it's the hit of the table. Let the people put on their own salt or salt it just before serving. Get some crisp bread for dunking cause OOH it's so GOOD!!™

Tired of tossed green salad — try tomatoes and onions — your family will think you're so smart. Try it with crispy bread to soak up the juice!

Mushroom Hungarian

makes 12 servings

2 lbs.	fresh mushrooms
¼ cup	butter or margarine
½ cup	finely chopped onion
1 Tbsp.	flour
1 Tbsp.	paprika
1½ tsp.	lemon juice
1 tsp.	salt
	dash ground red pepper
1 cup	sour cream

Rinse, pat dry, and slice fresh mushrooms. Set aside. In a large skillet, melt butter. Add onion and sauté three minutes; do not brown. Then add mushrooms and sauté 3 minutes, stirring occasionally. Stir in flour, paprika, lemon juice, salt and red pepper. Cook another 3 minutes, stirring occasionally. Add sour cream. Heat but do not boil. Serve over toast points if desired or add steak or chicken strips.

So easy and versatile, 'cause it's a side dish, sauce or even a main dish! A quick winner any way you use it!

BREADS

*Before we get to the full-fledged desserts —
here's a few called breads that are really
desserts in bread shape.*

*All of them are mixing and baking. No
punching, rolling, proofing, or any of that —
they're simple and no-fail. What a home touch
they are for snacking, or for dessert, or for a
meal accompaniment.*

*All of them go well with butter, cream cheese or
"as they are" — and they are all "easy
winners."*

Easy Pumpkin Bread

Don't wait for pumpkin season to make — it's too delicious for waiting.

1½ cups	sugar
1¼ cups	flour
1 cup	canned pumpkin
½ cup	salad oil
½ cup	raisins
½ cup	walnuts (broken ones are fine)
⅓ cup	water
2	eggs
1 tsp.	baking soda
½ tsp.	allspice
½ tsp.	cinnamon
½ tsp.	nutmeg
¼ tsp.	baking powder

Combine in a bowl and mix well. Pour into a greased loaf baking pan and bake for an hour and a quarter (75 minutes) in a preheated 350° oven or until it tests done. Let cool and enjoy 'cause OOH it's so GOOD!!™

Just mix and bake. Pumpkin or cake has never been better. You can't fail with this recipe. Is this ever a winner!! You'll love it!

Livery Stable Strawberry Bread

makes two 9×5 inch loaves

This is one of my first TV Biggies.

2 cups	frozen unsweetened whole strawberries
	sugar
3 cups plus 2 Tbsp.	all purpose flour
2 cups	sugar
1 Tbsp.	cinnamon
1 tsp.	salt
1¼ cups	oil
4	eggs
1¼ cups	chopped pecans
1 tsp.	baking soda

Place strawberries in medium bowl. Sprinkle lightly with sugar. Let berries stand until thawed, then slice. Preheat oven to 350° F. Butter and flour two 9×5″ loaf pans. Combine flour, sugar, cinnamon, salt and baking soda in large bowl and mix well. Blend oil and eggs into strawberries. Add to flour mixture. Stir in pecans, blending until dry ingredients are just moistened. Divide batter between pans. Bake loaves until tester inserted in center comes out clean, about 45 to 50 minutes. Let cool in pans on rack for 10 minutes. Turn loaves out and cool completely.

Have some extra fresh strawberries starting to go soft? This came from the Miami Herald *food section, one of my favorite food columns.*

Applesauce 'n Spice Bread

Crunchy outside; moist inside. Makes a perfect gift bread.

2 cups	all-purpose flour
1 tsp.	baking soda
½ tsp.	baking powder
½ tsp.	cinnamon
¼ tsp.	salt
¼ tsp.	nutmeg
¼ tsp.	allspice
1 cup	sugar
½ cup	vegetable oil
2	eggs
1¼ cups	sweetened applesauce
3 Tbsp.	milk
½ cup	coarsely chopped pecans
	Topping
¼ cup	chopped pecans
¼ cup	packed brown sugar
½ tsp.	cinnamon

Sift flour with baking soda, baking powder, salt and spices. Combine sugar, oil, applesauce, eggs and milk. Add sifted dry ingredients and nuts. Pour batter into greased 9 × 5 × 3″ loaf pan. Mix topping ingredients thoroughly and sprinkle over batter. Bake at 350° F. for 1 to 1¼ hours. OOH it's so GOOD!!™

Make a bunch and keep some in the freezer. My kind of baking — simple and no fail — plus it tastes like it's right from the tree.

Sweet Potato Muffins* *makes about 1 dozen*

1¾ cups	all-purpose flour
¼ cup	sugar
1 Tbsp.	baking powder
1 tsp.	salt
¾ cup	coarsely chopped almonds, toasted
1¼ cups	cooked, mashed sweet potatoes
¾ cup	milk
¼ cup	butter or margarine, melted
2	eggs, slightly beaten
¼ cup	sugar
½ tsp.	ground cinnamon

Combine first 5 ingredients in a large bowl, stirring well. Make a well in center of mixture. Combine next 4 ingredients, stirring well; add to dry ingredients, mixing just until moistened. Spoon batter into greased muffin pans, filling ¾ full. Combine ¼ cup sugar and cinnamon; sprinkle over each muffin. Bake at 425° for 25 to 30 minutes.

*From *Creative Ideas* magazine.

Try them just plain, or with honey, or cream cheese, or maple syrup, or butter or jelly, or??

Carrot Muffins*

makes about 1 dozen

1 (8¼ oz.) can	crushed pineapple, undrained
	milk
2 cups	all-purpose flour
⅓ cup	firmly packed brown sugar
1 Tbsp.	baking powder
½ tsp.	salt
2 Tbsp.	sugar
½ tsp.	ground cinnamon
¾ cup	grated carrots
⅓ cup	vegetable oil
1	egg, beaten
½ tsp.	vanilla extract

Drain pineapple, reserving juice. Add enough milk to the pineapple juice to measure ¾ cup liquid. Set aside. Combine next 7 ingredients in a large bowl, stirring until carrots are well coated; make a well in center of mixture. Combine pineapple, milk mixture, oil, egg and vanilla; add to dry ingredients, mixing just until moistened. Spoon batter into greased muffin pans, filling ¾ full. Bake muffins at 375° for 25 to 30 minutes or until done.

*From *Creative Ideas* magazine

Actually they're little individual carrot cakes! Moist, rich and scrumptious!

DESSERTS

Why are there a few more desserts here than any of the other categories?

'Cause that's what people request more than any other category — they're by far and away the favorites.

It seems no matter how much we cut down on anything else, it's probably so that we can still have our dessert. Well, it's always so pleasant to eat and the last course of the meal to be remembered — make it a good one, capable of making you a hero.

These are the "Biggies" — all of them quick, easy, and sensible — most of them can be whipped up in hardly any time at all — and every one a luscious winner — And I know; I've made every one. (And eaten them, too.)

Enjoy!!

Key Lime Pie

1 (15 oz.) can	sweetened condensed milk
1 Tbsp.	grated key lime rind
½ cup	key lime juice
2	slightly beaten egg yolks
1	graham cracker crust

Mix milk, rind and egg yolks. Add lime juice, stirring as you add; continue stirring until thickened. Thickening is a result of the reaction of the milk with the lime juice. Chill for 3 hours. Serve plain or with whipped cream.

No cooking. Throw together. Tastes just like Florida — Yippee! I use a bought crust from the market — Then it's even easier —

Apple Cinnamon Rolls   *makes 4-6 servings*

2	large apples, peeled and cored
1	can refrigerated quick crescent dinner rolls
2 Tbsp.	butter or margarine, melted
½ cup	sugar
1 tsp.	cinnamon
¼ cup	orange juice or water

Preheat oven to 400°. Cut each apple into eight pieces. Unroll crescent roll dough; separate into eight triangles. Cut each in half lengthwise to make 16 triangle strips. Place an apple piece at wide end of each strip; roll up. Arrange in baking dish. Drizzle with butter; sprinkle with mixture of sugar and cinnamon. Pour orange juice or water into pan, but not over dumplings. Bake at 400° for 30 to 35 minutes or until apples are tender. Serve warm, plain or with cream.

OOH it's so GOOD!!™

Quick Apple No Pie

Peel and cut up 4 or 5 good size apples in ½ inch wedges, place into a skillet into which you have melted 4 tablespoons of margarine (or butter) and add a tablespoon of lemon juice. Coat the apples by turning. Mix in 1 teaspoon of apple pie spice and 4 tablespoons of light brown sugar and a pinch of salt. Turn stove to medium heat and cook until apples are starting to soften. Stir them lightly a couple of times; it only takes 5 to 7 minutes. Spoon apples into small bowls and serve with your favorite topping. Yes you can serve it cooled also.

Suggestions: Some people like to add to the skillet 2 tablespoons of grape nuts or 2 or 3 crushed graham crackers. If the apple pie spice is unavailable use a combination of ¾ teaspoon cinnamon and ¼ teaspoon nutmeg.

Served in a bowl with ice cream or whipped cream or maybe a slice of cheddar cheese will give it that fancy look.

Pumpkin Praline Pie
makes 1 9" pie

2 cups	cooked, mashed pumpkin
1 (14 oz.) can	sweetened condensed milk
2	eggs
1 tsp.	ground cinnamon
½ tsp.	ground nutmeg
½ tsp.	ground ginger
½ tsp.	salt
1	unbaked 9-inch pastry shell
12 to 14	pecan halves
3 Tbsp.	dark brown sugar
3 Tbsp.	whipping cream

Combine pumpkin, condensed milk, eggs, spices and salt; beat on medium speed of an electric mixer one minute or until smooth. Pour into pastry shell; bake at 375° for 50 minutes or until knife inserted halfway between center and edge of pie comes out clean. Let cool slightly; arrange pecan halves in a circle on top of pie, and set aside.

Combine sugar and whipping cream in a small saucepan; cook over medium heat, stirring constantly, until sugar dissolves. Reduce heat, and simmer 5 minutes, let cool 5 minutes. Spoon over pecan halves.

Pumpkin at its very best. Pumpkin tangy and pumpkin smooth all in one.

Apricot Cream Cheese Pie

1½ lbs.	cream cheese
4	eggs
½ lb.	sugar
1½ tsp.	vanilla
2 (1 lb.) cans	apricot halves, drained
2	graham cracker pie shells (9-inch)
	whipped cream as desired

Combine cream cheese, eggs, sugar, vanilla and 1 lb. of canned apricot halves in mixer; beat at medium speed 3 minutes or until thoroughly blended. Pour ingredients into pie shells. Bake in preheated 350° oven 50 minutes. Chill. Garnish with remaining apricot halves and whipped cream, if desired.

> *The apricots are so good!! But if you make it with peaches, it's good too!! This recipe's enough for 2 pies, so invite the neighbors!*

Platte County Pie

2	large eggs
½ cup	flour
1 cup	sugar
1 tsp.	vanilla
½ cup	softened butter
½ cup	pecans
1 cup	semi-sweet chocolate chips
1	pie shell

Beat eggs, add flour and sugar, butter, nuts and chocolate chips. Pour into pie shell. Bake 1 hour at 325°.

> *From the* Miami Herald. *Just beat and mix together and you've got a sinfully rich chocolate chip pie. Oh, do I use this often! Fits my basic easy-but-scrumptious requirements.*

Quick Mud Pie

1	store-bought chocolate cookie crust or 30 crushed chocolate wafer cookies
⅔ stick	butter or margarine softened
½ gal.	your favorite ice cream, softened enough to spread into pie crust (coffee is the traditional flavor, but your family may have a particular favorite)
1 pkg.	premade hot fudge topping (don't warm it) whipped topping or real whipped cream if you prefer chopped nuts (for sprinkling)

Crush the chocolate cookies and mix with the softened butter. Press into the bottom and sides of a glass pie plate. Cool until firm. Spoon in the softened ice cream, top it with lacework of fudge topping and freeze well. Done. Put on whipped topping and crushed nuts after cutting into slices and yummy. OOH it's so GOOD!!™

Could become a family classic, but the best part is there's no cooking, no mess and it's quick.

French Silk Pie

4	egg yolks
¼ box (4 oz.)	powdered confectioner's sugar
½ lb.	softened unsalted butter
⅓ cup	Kahlua®
1	banana
1 oz.	Amaretto
1	graham cracker pie crust

In a bowl, place the egg yolks, powdered sugar, butter and Kahlua®. These should be at room temperature, not cold. In the meantime, thinly slice the banana and cover the bottom of the graham cracker crust. Sprinkle the Amaretto over the bananas and let soak into crust.

With an electric beater, whip at high speed the eggs, sugar, butter and Kahlua® for about 10 minutes (this is important for consistency and texture). Place in crust and refrigerate. Serve with homemade whipped cream and chocolate shavings.

Oh, will this ever be the hit of the party! Cut the pieces small, though. It's rich, rich, rich! It's simple, smooth, unique, and so fancy — yet it's easy and quick with no cooking — what a combo!

Chocolate Chip Almond Pie

6	small chocolate bars with almonds
17	marshmallows
½ cup	milk
1 cup	whipping cream, whipped
½ cup	chocolate chips
½ cup	slivered almonds
1	baked graham cracker crust

Melt chocolate bars and marshmallows in milk in top of a double boiler; cool. Fold in whipped cream, chocolate chips, and slivered almonds. Pour into graham cracker crust. Garnish with additional chocolate chips. Refrigerate for at least 4 hours.

This is made from your favorite chocolate bar and it's chocolate bar delicious (and easy). Everybody will be oohing and ahhing all over the place thinking that you're a wonder when only you know how easy it was!

Simple Pecan Pie

1 cup	sugar
6 tsp.	melted butter or margarine
3	eggs, beaten
½ cup	dark corn syrup
1 tsp.	vanilla
1 cup	pecans

Beat eggs thoroughly with sugar, corn syrup, melted butter or margarine and vanilla. Add pecans. Pour into unbaked 9″ pie shell. Bake at 350° for 45 minutes to an hour, or until knife inserted halfway between outside and center comes out clean.

If you thought pecan pie was hard to make, this sure proves how easy it really is. It's easy, easy, easy! You certainly don't want to do any more than you have to in the kitchen — that's why we call it "simple."

Toll House Golden Brownies

makes 35 2″ squares

2 cups	unsifted flour
2 tsp.	baking powder
1 tsp.	salt
¾ cup	butter, softened
¾ cup	sugar
¾ cup	firmly packed dark brown sugar
1 tsp.	vanilla extract
3	eggs
1 (12 oz.) pkg.	Nestle Toll House Morsels

Preheat oven to 350° F. In small bowl, combine flour, baking powder and salt; set aside. In large bowl, combine butter, sugar, dark brown sugar and vanilla extract; beat until creamy. Add eggs, one at a time, beating well after each addition. Gradually add flour mixture; mix well. Stir in Nestle Toll House Morsels.

Spread evenly into well-greased 15″ × 10″ × 1″ baking pan. Bake at 350° for 30-35 minutes. Cool; cut into 2″ squares.

You're supposed to get 35 - 2″ squares — but for some reason we never wind up with that many on the platter! Especially when we leave the room for a few minutes — can't figure it out!

Caramel Brownies

1 (14 oz.) pkg.	light caramels
⅔ cup	evaporated milk
1 (18¼ oz.) pkg.	German chocolate cake mix (almost any kind of chocolate cake mix will work)
¾ cup	melted margarine
1 cup	chopped pecans
6 oz.	semi-sweet chocolate chips

Melt the caramels with ⅓ cup evaporated milk. Combine in a bowl the cake mix, margarine, ⅓ cup evaporated milk and the pecans. Stir with spoon until dough holds together. Grease and flour a 13″ × 9″ pan. Press half the dough into pan. Bake at 350° for 6 minutes. Remove pan and pour chocolate chips over baked dough. Spread melted caramels over chips and cover with other half of the dough. Bake 20 minutes. Cool in refrigerator 30 minutes before cutting.

OOH it's so GOOD!!™ | *A delicious taste treat for not only the kids, but the whole family!*

Chewy Chocolate Chippers
makes about 2 dozen, 3½″ cookies

1 cup	butter or margarine
1½ cups	firmly packed light brown sugar
2	eggs
1 tsp.	vanilla
2¼ cups	flour
1 tsp.	baking soda
½ tsp.	salt
1 cup	"M & M's" plain chocolate candies
½ cup	chopped nuts

Beat together butter and sugar until light and fluffy; blend in eggs and vanilla. Gradually add combined flour, soda and salt; mix well. Stir in candies and nuts. Drop dough by heaping tablespoonsful onto greased cookie sheet about 3″ apart. Press 2 to 3 additional candies into each cookie, if desired. Bake at 350° F. for 9 to 11 minutes or until lightly browned. Cool on cookie sheet about 3 minutes; remove cookies to wire rack to cool thoroughly.

It's a chewy chocolate chip cookie that will have the kids begging you for more and more!

Peanut Butter Chocolate Candy Cookies

Mix together:

1 cup	peanut butter
2 sticks	melted margarine
1 lb. box	confectioners sugar
1 cup	crushed graham crackers (or graham cracker crumbs)

Put this mixture into a well-greased cookie sheet and pour over it a 12 oz. bag of melted chocolate morsels. Refrigerate for 15 minutes. Remove and slice into 2″ × 2″ squares. Leave in pan and put back in refrigerator. Serve cold.

Fantastic!!!

This is the all time winner for requests for a recipe. No cooking, just enjoying. Tastes like peanut butter cups. There's no such thing as making too many of these! My favorite combination — peanut butter and chocolate! The perfect treat or snack for every kid under 90!

Date Nut Bars

1 cup	flour
½ cup	sugar
½ tsp.	each: nutmeg and baking powder
¼ tsp.	salt
¼ cup	oil
2	eggs
1 Tbsp.	lemon juice
1 (8 oz.) pkg.	chopped dates
1 cup	walnuts, chopped
	Topping:
1 Tbsp.	sugar mixed with ½ tsp. nutmeg

In 9″ square pan mix well flour, sugar, nutmeg, baking powder and salt. Add oil, eggs and lemon juice. With rubber spatula, mix and stir until well blended. (Batter will be thick.) Stir in dates and nuts. Bake in preheated 350° oven about 30 minutes or until lightly browned and pick inserted in center comes out clean. Sprinkle with topping. Cool in pan on rack. Cut in 4″ × 1″ bars or 2-inch squares. Makes 16.

From Woman's Day Magazine

These are the ones that you'd devour with cold glasses of milk or rich coffee. You guessed it — with anything. The company knows it's homemade. My kind of cookie is one where there's really something to dig your teeth into. So simple, you don't even have to wash the cooking pan until the cake is all eaten!

Sun-Maid Raisin Oaties   *makes about 36 cookies*

Create these delicious raisin oatmeal cookies with fresh, sweet Sun-Maid Raisins. And bake up some smiles

1 cup	butter or margarine
¾ cup	granulated sugar
¾ cup	packed brown sugar
2	eggs
1½ tsp.	vanilla
2 cups	all-purpose flour
1 tsp.	salt
1 tsp.	baking soda
2 cups	old-fashioned oats
1 cup	Sun-Maid Raisins

Cream together butter, sugars, eggs and vanilla. Stir in flour, salt, baking soda and oats; mix well. Stir in raisins. Drop by tablespoonsful onto lightly greased baking sheets. Bake above oven center at 375°, 10 to 12 minutes or until lightly browned. Remove to wire racks to cool.

Home on a rainy day with the kids saying what are we gonna do?? Try oatmeal raisin cookies.

Chocolate Mayonnaise Cake

2 cups	unsifted flour
⅔ cup	unsweetened cocoa
1¼ tsp.	baking soda
¼ tsp.	baking powder
1⅔ cups	sugar
3	eggs
1 tsp.	vanilla
1 cup	Hellman's or Best Foods real mayonnaise
1⅓ cups	water

Grease and flour bottoms of 2 (9-inch) round baking pans. In medium bowl stir together first 4 ingredients; set aside. In large bowl with mixer at high speed beat next 3 ingredients, occasionally scraping bowl, 3 minutes or until light and fluffy. Reduce speed to low; beat in real mayonnaise. Add flour mixture in 4 additions alternately with water, beginning and ending with flour. Pour into prepared pans. Bake in 350° oven 30 to 35 minutes or until cake tester inserted in center comes out clean. Cool in pans 10 minutes. Remove, cool on wire racks. Frost as desired. Garnish with sliced almonds.

This is the original rich chocolate tasting cake you remember from the old fashioned days. After this, there's no other chocolate cake. Wait and see! Chocolate mayonnaise sounds funny, I know, but wait till you taste it.

Lemon Squares

Crust:		Filling:	
2 cups	sifted flour	4	eggs, beaten well
½ cup	powdered sugar	2 cups	sugar
½ lb.	soft margarine	3 level Tbsp.	flour
		½ tsp.	baking powder
		5 Tbsp.	lemon juice

Mix flour and powdered sugar. Cut in margarine, pat into greased 9" × 13" pan. Bake in 350° oven, 15-20 minutes. Beat eggs; add sugar, flour, baking powder and lemon juice. Pour on hot crust. Bake another 20 minutes. Remove and spread powdered sugar over cake; cut while warm, not hot or cool. Refrigerate and serve.

> *It's meringuey, puddingy and cakey all in one. Cut a little larger and served with whipped cream, it's a perfect lemon torte dessert all year through — but summer? Gangbusters!*

Crustless Cheese Cake

2 (8 oz.) pkgs.	cream cheese	Topping	
⅔ cup	sugar	16 oz.	sour cream
3	eggs	3 Tbsp.	sugar
½ tsp.	vanilla	1 tsp.	vanilla
¼ tsp.	lemon juice (fresh)	¼ tsp.	lemon juice

Soften cream cheese and beat with sugar very well. Add eggs one at a time. Add ½ teaspoon of vanilla, ¼ teaspoon lemon juice, mix well. Put the mixture into a greased glass pie plate. Bake at 325° 50 minutes until brown. Remove from oven. Cool for 10 to 15 minutes.

Topping
Mix all topping ingredients together. Spread over top of pie. Bake again for 10 minutes. The top will be almost liquid but cool it and put in the refrigerator for 4 hours or overnight.

> *No crust, no rolling, no mess! This was the very first MR. FOOD® TV sensation!*

Gayle's 7-Up Cake

1½ cups	butter
3 cups	sugar
5	eggs
3 cups	flour
2 Tbsp.	lemon extract
¾ cup	7-Up

Cream sugar and butter until light and fluffy. Add eggs, one at a time, beating well after each addition. Add flour. Beat in lemon extract and 7-Up. Pour batter into well greased and floured jumbo fluted mold (such as a bundt pan). Bake 1½ - 1¾ hours at 325°. Remove from pan 10 to 15 minutes after being taken out of oven. Serve with lemon sherbet.

Can add grated lemon rind to enhance lemon flavor. Can dust with powdered sugar. Enjoy — cause, OOH it's so GOOD!!™

> *Yes — that's right — 7-Up is the secret ingredient — and you'll love it. This is a moist pound cake type cake that can be used year round for snacking, shortcake, stacking, anything — best all round cake.*

Creamy Rice Pudding

makes 4 servings

2 cups	cooked rice
2 cups	milk
4½ Tbsp.	sugar
	dash of salt
1 Tbsp.	butter or margarine
½ tsp.	vanilla

Combine rice, milk, sugar, salt and butter. Cook over medium heat until thickened (about 20 minutes) stirring often. Add vanilla. OOH it's so GOOD!!™

> *Creamy type is my favorite. It's like a rice, custard pudding . . . so smooth I could eat a gallon a sitting. I'd like to, but I don't.*

Rice Heavenly Hash

makes 12 servings

2 cups	cooked rice
1½ cups	milk
¼ cup	sugar
1 cup	drained, canned pineapple tidbits
1	large orange, peeled, seeded and diced
¼ cup	chopped maraschino cherries
1 cup	miniature marshmallows
½ cup	flaked coconut
¼ cup	nut meats, chopped
1 envelope	whipped topping mix, prepared

Combine rice, milk, and sugar. Cook until thick and creamy, about 10 to 15 minutes, stirring occasionally. Cool. Fold in remaining ingredients. Spoon into serving dishes and chill. Garnish with additional maraschino cherries, if desired. OOH it's so GOOD!!™

> *It's the perfect anytime summer dessert cause it just oozes with the pleasures of the tropics! It's actually a fast, creamy rice pudding!*

Fruit Compote

A "Fruit Compote" is a light dessert. Rinse 2½ cups dried, pitted prunes. Drain. Place prunes, slices from 4 peeled oranges, 2 cups of water and ⅓ cup of sugar in large casserole. Cover and bake in 350°F oven about 40 minutes. Serve warm with molasses cookies.

> *Easy compote for light spring dessert. Careful — don't overcook the fruit. We want it to be a little solid.*

Grapenut Pudding

1 cup	Grape-nuts
2 cups	milk (heated)
2 cups	half and half
4	eggs beaten
½ cup	sugar
¼ tsp.	salt
1 tsp.	vanilla
	nutmeg

Combine all ingredients, except nutmeg. Make as custard. Butter 9″ × 9″ baking dish, pour in custard, sprinkle nutmeg on top. Set baking dish in pan of water. (Be careful don't let the water overflow when you put the custard dish in.) Cook in oven 350° for 2-2½ hours, or until inserted toothpick comes out dry.

Easy, sweet, mellow, crunchy, you just can't miss with all that going for it. A New England favorite for many, many, many years.

Crystal Pineapple Sherbet *makes 2 servings*

1 (8 oz.) can	Dole chunk pineapple in heavy syrup
2 tsp.	orange-flavored liqueur
1 tsp.	minced crystalized ginger
2 tsp.	diced pistachio nuts

Freeze unopened pineapple overnight. At least 20 minutes before serving remove pineapple from freezer. Open can and break pineapple in can with fork. Add liqueur and ginger to blender. Add half the frozen pineapple; whirl until mixed. Stir, add remaining pineapple; whirl, turning blender on and off until smooth. Stir when necessary. Spoon mixture into wine glasses. Top each with pistachios.

Unexpected company? What an easy, rave-getting dessert. You're never caught short without a dessert 'cause it can be whipped up into a winner in minutes.

Fried Bananas

for six bananas in chunks

Batter: mix together adding liquid items to dry items

1	egg
½ cup	water
1 cup	corn starch ⎱
1 cup	sifted flour ⎰ OR
½ tsp.	salt
1 cup	coconut cream
1 Tbsp.	melted butter
¼ tsp.	baking powder

¾ cup	rice flour
¼ cup	sticky rice flour (yes, that's 1 cup rather than 2 for total)

Dip banana chunks into batter and fry in hot oil until golden.

> *For the most eaten fresh fruit in the country — a new way to be prepared. Serve it as an appetizer, a side dish or a dessert!*

Banana in Chocolate Sauce

makes 4 servings

¾ cup	sugar
1½ Tbsp.	unsalted butter
2 oz. (2 squares)	unsweetened baking chocolate, broken up
½ cup	heavy cream
½ tsp.	vanilla extract
4	firm bananas, sliced on the diagonal

In a heavy medium saucepan, combine the sugar, butter, chocolate, and cream. Cook over moderate heat, stirring constantly, until the mixture blends and comes to a boil. Let boil gently, without stirring, for 2 minutes. Remove from the heat and stir in the vanilla. Arrange the banana slices on 4 dessert plates. Spoon the chocolate sauce over the bananas while it is still hot.

> *Caught without dessert for a special or unannounced dinner — here's the answer for you. Add a strawberry, some cake crumbs or chopped nuts — there's no limit to how simple or fancy you can make it.*

Kiwifruit Gelato

makes about 2⅓ cups

1 cup	water
½ cup	sugar
½ cup	light corn syrup
3-4	California kiwifruit, pared
5 tsp.	lemon or lime juice
¼ tsp.	grated lemon or lime peel

Combine water, sugar and corn syrup in saucepan. Cook and stir two minutes or until sugar is dissolved. Puree kiwifruit in food processor or blender to equal ¾ cup puree. Add lemon juice, lemon peel and sugar mixture. Pour into shallow metal pan; freeze one hour or until firm but not solid. Spoon into chilled bowl and beat with electric mixer until light and fluffy; return to pan. Return to freezer; freeze about two hours or until firm enough to scoop.

Tip: Kiwifruit gelato can be frozen in an ice cream freezer according to manufacturer's directions.

> *The most delicious ices (excuse me, Gelato) to fancy up your table. Gelato is what we used to call ices — either way a refreshing taste treat!*

Raspberry Cream

makes 4 servings

1 (10 oz.) pkg.	frozen raspberries, partially thawed
½ cup	confectioners sugar
½ cup	heavy cream
2 Tbsp.	lemon juice
1 Tbsp.	chopped nuts

Whip raspberries, confectioners sugar, heavy cream and lemon juice in blender until smooth. Pour into 4 individual dessert dishes; sprinkle with nuts.

> *I've got a dandy June July August Treat that looks cool, tastes cool and keeps us cool! Serve with melon chunks for a summer delight!*

Italian Christmas Cream
makes 8 to 10 servings

2	medium, firm Dole bananas, peeled, sliced
1 cup	sliced green grapes
1 (16 oz.) carton	dairy sour cream
1 cup	coarsely chopped maraschino cherries
1 cup	coarsely chopped walnuts
½ cup	sugar
1½ tsp.	fresh grated lemon peel

Combine all ingredients until well mixed. Pour into 2-quart shallow casserole dish or mold. Freeze overnight. Stand at room temperature 15 to 20 minutes before cutting or unmolding. Cut into 8 or 10 squares or slices.

A little something to add to the specialness of Christmas! Here's a little secret — You don't have to wait until Christmas to enjoy this special treat!

Chocolate Mousse
makes 6 servings

4	eggs, separated
1 (6 oz.) pkg.	semi-sweet chocolate pieces
5 Tbsp.	boiling coffee
2 Tbsp.	orange-flavored liqueur (optional)

Beat egg whites in a medium size bowl with electric mixer until soft peaks form. Place chocolate pieces in container of electric blender. Whirl to break up pieces. Add boiling coffee; whirl until smooth. Add egg yolks and liqueur. Whirl 1 minute or until well blended. Fold chocolate mixture into beaten egg whites until no streaks of white remain. Spoon into six dessert dishes. Chill.

No cook chocolate mousse — just mixing — it can't be easier! Use your favorite orange flavored liqueur to make it oh so fancy!

HODGE PODGE

I didn't know where to put these, so I made up a Hodge Podge section — and the reason that I just had to use them is that they are so great — ones that I use as standards as often as I can, (they are that good) but had no separate section of their own —

Except, Hodge Podge!

See for yourself.

Blue Cheese Dressing

1½ cups	sour cream
¼ cup	mayonnaise
1 Tbsp.	oil
1 Tbsp.	white vinegar
	dash pepper
4 oz.	blue cheese
	salt to taste

Put all ingredients in blender. Blend to desired consistency. Add salt to taste if needed. More cheese too, if needed.

When you want to make a special blue cheese dressing (rather than one of the regular bought ones), here's the easiest way to do it. You can add more of any of the ingredients if you want, but try it this way first. After it's blended, I put in a couple ounces more of crumbled blue cheese to give it a chunk effect.

Creamy Fruit Dressing

1 cup	mayonnaise
1 cup	dairy sour cream
6 Tbsp.	frozen pineapple juice (concentrate, thawed)
4 Tbsp.	confectioners sugar
4 Tbsp.	grated orange peel (fresh is best, but dried is ok, too)
	dash of Allspice

Mix all ingredients together well in a bowl. Serve over fresh cut fruit. It's immediately fancy — and OOH it's so GOOD!!™

Fancy up your old fruit cup. Serve it over any type or combination of fruit! It makes a nice dip for fruit slices, chunks also.

Creamy Pepper Dressing *makes approx. 3 cups*

2 cups	mayonnaise
½ cup	milk
¼ cup	water
2 Tbsp.	freshly grated parmesan cheese
1 Tbsp.	freshly ground pepper
1 Tbsp.	cider vinegar
1 tsp.	fresh lemon juice
1 tsp.	finely chopped onion
1 tsp.	garlic salt
1 dash	red pepper sauce
1 dash	Worcestershire sauce

Whisk all ingredients until well combined. Chill well before serving.

> *The best, best, best — not only my favorite salad dressing, but a base for adding other seasonings like garlic for garlic dressing, dill for dill dressing, etc.*

Louis Dressing

1 cup	mayonnaise
¼ cup	sour cream
½ cup	chili sauce (ketchup type)
2	hard cooked eggs, chopped
¼ cup	finely chopped scallions (or onions)
2 Tbsp.	stuffed green olives, chopped
⅛ tsp.	salt
⅛ tsp.	pepper

Mix well, all ingredients together in a bowl. Great for over seafood salad or even green salad. Enjoy!

> *A very elegant, fancy way to serve shrimp, crab or any seafood salad. Very similar to a 1000 Island Dressing — only fancier and thicker. Try some of your own favorite seasonings like tarragon or horseradish for a change.*

Colorful Antipasto Salad

½ cup	salad oil
½ cup	red wine vinegar
4 Tbsp.	finely chopped onion
4 Tbsp.	finely chopped parsley
2	crushed cloves garlic
1½ tsp.	sugar
½ tsp.	salt
	black pepper to taste
2	green peppers cut into eighths
2	red peppers cut into eighths
½ lb.	thickly sliced mushrooms
1 cup	pitted olives

Toss all ingredients well. Refrigerate overnight.

A simple just mix together antipasto salad that could be the centerpiece of your table, it's that colorful. Try your own favorite selection of veggies!

Cabbage Salad Cole Slaw

3 cups	shredded cabbage
1 tsp.	prepared mustard
1 Tbsp.	water
6 Tbsp.	vegetable oil
2 Tbsp.	sugar
½ tsp.	onion powder
½ tsp.	salt
½ tsp.	celery seed

In mixing bowl, mix together all ingredients except shredded cabbage. Then toss mixture with the cabbage, add 3 tablespoons vinegar. Toss again, chill enjoy. Adjust seasoning to your taste more, less, or different. Everything works.

Counting calories? There's no mayonnaise in this coleslaw! I realize everyone in the world has their own BEST coleslaw recipe — but once in a while you might want to try something different! You can even buy packages of shredded cabbage to save even more time!

Tempura Batter for Veggies

1½ cups	flour
½ cup	corn starch
¼ cup	baking powder
1 Tbsp.	sugar
1 tsp.	salt
½ tsp.	pepper
⅛ tsp.	cayenne pepper (optional)
2½ cups	water

Add dry ingredients together, then add 2½ cups water and mix together. Cover with foil — not tightly, just loosely on top. Let stand on kitchen counter for 2 to 3 hours. Dip vegetables into a little corn starch, then into the batter and fry in about ¾ inch of hot oil until golden. Turn them with tongs carefully (to get both sides). It only takes minutes.

By the way, if you like garlic?? A ½ teaspoon in that batter is the greatest. Enjoy!! Cause, OOH it's so GOOD!!™

> *Tempura is the rage way to enjoy crispy cooked vegetables! Choose your favorite veggies for your tempura! They all work nicely.*

Burgundy Cooler

1 bottle	(5th) Taylor Burgundy chilled (or any brand)
¼ cup	fresh lime juice
3 (7 oz.) bottles	Seven Up chilled or any brand lemon flavored soft drink

Combine ingredients in a 2 quart pitcher. Pour into tall, ice filled glasses. Garnish with fresh lime slice.

Enjoy!

> *This is as rewarding as any Sangria. Nice for that summer garden party, but, remember NO DRINKING AND DRIVING! It's good old summer easy lazy day time!*

Harpoon

makes 1 drink

4	canned cling peach slices
½ cup	cranberry juice cocktail
1½ oz.	light rum
½ tsp.	granulated sugar
½ cup	bar ice
1	maraschino cherry

Whirl in blender 3 peach slices, cranberry juice, rum, and sugar until frothy. Skewer remaining peach slice and maraschino cherry and use as garnish. OOH it's so GOOD!!™

Want people to say "Gee that's delicious, I'll have some of that" — then here's a drink recipe for you! Serve it in your favorite glassware to make it soooo fancy!

Blender Fruit Drink

1 (29 oz.) can	fruit cocktail
½ cup	sour cream
4 Tbsp.	Grenadine
2 cups	fresh, diced fruit

Just whirl it in the blender until smooth. Easy, wasn't it? Serve chilled.

You might want to add a few tablespoons of sugar to sweeten it and the juice of half a lemon or lime along with the sugar. Play with it to get it your favorite way. Enjoy!! Cause OOH it's so GOOD!!™

Here's a way to empty the bottom of your fruit bin and use up all those over ripened fruit! It's a refreshing drink or a super chilled soup first course! Or freeze it on a stick like the new frozen fruit sticks.

TO ORDER SEND TO:
Mr. Food® Cookbook, OOH it's so GOOD!!™
Clearing House, P.O. Box 3000, Troy, NY 12180

Please send me _____ copies of Mr. Food® Cookbook at $8.95 each plus
$1.50 each for postage and handling.

Enclosed is my check or money order for $ _____ made payable to Mr. Food®
Cookbook. New York State residents add 7% ($.63) sales tax per copy.

PLEASE ALLOW 4-6 WEEKS FOR DELIVERY.

CREDIT CARD: ☐ VISA ☐ MASTER CARD

ACCOUNT #

EXPIRATION DATE _____

SEND TO: (Please print.)

NAME

ADDRESS

CITY   STATE   ZIP

SIGNATURE

- -

Get an extra copy 'cause,

it's an anytime little present that tells someone that you
want them to say. . .

OOH it's so GOOD!! ™

- -

TO ORDER SEND TO:
Mr. Food® Cookbook, OOH it's so GOOD!!™
Clearing House, P.O. Box 3000, Troy, NY 12180

Please send me _____ copies of Mr. Food® Cookbook at $8.95 each plus
$1.50 each for postage and handling.

Enclosed is my check or money order for $ _____ made payable to Mr. Food®
Cookbook. New York State residents add 7% ($.63) sales tax per copy.

PLEASE ALLOW 4-6 WEEKS FOR DELIVERY.

CREDIT CARD: ☐ VISA ☐ MASTER CARD

ACCOUNT #

EXPIRATION DATE _____

SEND TO: (Please print.)

NAME

ADDRESS

CITY   STATE   ZIP

SIGNATURE

Have fun in the kitchen—
Play with your spice rack—
A sharp knife cuts easier than a dull one—
Enjoy! Enjoy!